narada's way of divine love

A gift from
Macaya Miracle

MacayaMiracle.com

Narada's Way of Divine Love

THE BHAKTI SUTRAS

TRANSLATION AND COMMENTARY BY

Swami Prabhavananda

Introduction by Christopher Isherwood

Vedanta Press
Hollywood, California

Vedanta Press
Hollywood, CA
Tel: (323) 960-1728

First paperback edition published 2000
Printed in the United States of America

Cover Design: Joan Greenblatt

ISBN: 0-87481-054-X
Library of Congress Catalog Number 75-161488

Readers interested in the subject material of this book are invited to write
to The Secretary, 1946 Vedanta Place, Hollywood CA 90068,
or e-mail us at info@vedanta.org.

Visit our websites:
www.vedanta.com • www.vedanta.org

The best path to union with God is to follow the way of divine love as taught by Narada.

SRI RAMAKRISHNA

CONTENTS

PREFACE

I HAVE DRAWN inspiration for this commentary from the teachings of Sri Ramakrishna and from the lives of his disciples, with most of whom it was my blessed fortune to be intimately associated. I have witnessed how these men of God showed forth in their own lives the knowledge and love of God which Narada described thousands of years ago, thus proving that his teachings are equally valid for us in this age.

SWAMI PRABHAVANANDA

HOLLYWOOD, CALIFORNIA
JANUARY 1971

INTRODUCTION

NARADA TELLS US that "the path of devotion is the easiest path to attain God."

"The path of devotion," called *bhakti yoga* in Sanskrit, is the approach to God through love. The *bhakta* makes a continual conscious effort to love God and to feel God's love for him. To this end, he repeats God's name and performs ritual worship. In order to have a particular object for his worship, he fixes his mind upon one chosen aspect of God or one out of the several divine incarnations. Narada, like the other great teachers, assures us however that, as the bhakta's devotion grows, he will become more and more aware that he is actually worshiping the God within himself which is his own true nature. In the supreme state of *bhakti*, worshiper and worshiped will be realized as one.

As defined by Hindu philosophy, there are four ways of attaining this unitive knowledge of God: *bhakti yoga, karma yoga, jnana yoga*, and *raja yoga*. Karma yoga is the approach to God through selfless action— action performed without desire for personal gain or fear of unpleasant consequences; it is often practiced by serving God through one's fellow men. Jnana yoga is the approach through discrimination between the real and the unreal; when all transitory phenomena have been rigorously analyzed and rejected, God alone remains and becomes known by a process of elimination. Raja yoga is the approach through intensive practice of meditation.

Now it is obvious that three of these *yogas* demand

qualities and powers which are not possessed by everyone or even by a large majority of human beings. Karma yoga calls for heroic energy as well as great humility and patience; jnana yoga for an exceptionally acute intellect; raja yoga for unwavering concentration and control of the senses. Compared with them, the practice of bhakti yoga appears far simpler, less austere and more inviting. Besides, while we may not flatter ourselves that we have exceptional energy, intellect or concentration, we are all firmly convinced that we are capable of love. Therefore we readily accept Narada's statement—that bhakti is the easiest of the yogas.

Too readily, in most cases. For do most of us realize what it is that we are accepting? Have we any idea at all what Narada means by loving God? Have we ever fully considered what we ourselves mean when we use, or misuse, the word "love"? Have we, indeed, ever truly loved anybody?

There is a phrase which was once current in everyday conversation and popular with song-writers: to be in love with love. When grown-ups were talking about the emotions of their teenage children they would say, with indulgent smiles, "Oh, she's just in love with love, that's all it is"—meaning that the teenager in question wasn't really in love but only indulging in romantic self-deception. *Real* love, the grown-ups implied, was something the teenagers would learn later, something adult and serious and down to earth—and there was a hint of grim satisfaction in their tone, as when combat veterans allude to what awaits a raw recruit.

The phrase has gone out of fashion but the attitude persists; real love is still defined in terms of the consequences and responsibilities it creates—social acceptance or disgrace, marriage or divorce, wealth or debts, childbearing or childlessness, domestic slavery or desertion. When people seem to be talking about love they are in fact discussing its consequences, more often than not. Indeed it is sometimes hard to see the love for the consequences. The relationship usually discussed is, of course, the sexual relationship. But no one can deny that the relations between parents and children, friends, colleagues, even animals and their owners, can become equally strained in times of crisis and create similar economic and social difficulties, similar torments of jealousy and merciless struggles of opposing egos.

There are many people, certainly, who manage to loosen the bonds of their own egotism enough to be able to love each other more or less unselfishly throughout their lives. Love, or at any rate the memory of love, is always present to some degree even in the unhappiest of relationships. And, as Narada reminds us, all love—no matter how the ego may distort or restrict it—is in essence divine. But the question remains, can a consideration of these states of imperfect human love be of any help to us in understanding the concept of bhakti yoga?

The love of God described by Narada is a love in which there can be no jealousy, no struggle of egos, no desire for material advantage or exclusive possession, no dread of desertion; a love which is incapable of unhappiness. Even the pain of temporary alienation from God cannot be called unhappy; for the devotee who feels it knows, simply because he does feel it, that God exists and that the relationship between them is alive and real.

But this concept of a love without unhappiness is just what we, as beginners in the study of bhakti, can scarcely grasp. That isn't love at all, we say to ourselves; it's cold, unnatural, inhuman. For we must admit, if we are frank, that we have become so conditioned by the world's view of love that we actually need to be made jealous, need to suffer craving and anxiety, need to make the hopeless demand for exclusive possession—because, without those familiar pains, we are unable to enjoy the respites from pain which we call happiness in love.

So perhaps there is still some usefulness in the old silly-sounding phrase; to be in love with love. Perhaps it can be helpful in giving us our first glimpse of what is meant by bhakti. Let us stop thinking of love as a relationship between two individual egos and concentrate on the capacity for love which is within each one of us. It may be very small but it is our own and it cannot fail us. We can all agree that our love, when it is thus regarded without relation to any external object, is both lovable for itself and completely free from desire or pain. And in this way we can begin to grasp the idea that love is God.

CHRISTOPHER ISHERWOOD

narada's way of divine love

NARADA

THE AUTHOR of the aphorisms contained in this book is Narada. But it is difficult to ascertain who Narada was. We find his name mentioned for the first time in the Chhandogya Upanishad, one of the ancient scriptures of the world. There we discover him as a spiritual aspirant approaching a great sage called Sanatkumar. Narada, we are told, had studied all the branches of learning—art, science, music, and philosophy, as well as the sacred scriptures. "But," he said to Sanatkumar, "I have gained no peace. I have studied all this, but the Self I do not know. I have heard from great teachers like you that he who knows the Self overcomes grief. Grief is ever my lot. Help me, I pray, to overcome it."

After some discussion between the master and the disciple, Sanatkumar taught him: "The Infinite is the source of joy. There is no joy in the finite. . . . The Infinite is immortal, the finite is mortal. . . . One who knows, meditates upon, and realizes the truth of the Self, the Infinite Being—such a one delights in the Self, revels in the Self, rejoices in the Self. He become master of himself and master of all the worlds. Slaves are they who know not this truth.

"When the senses are purified [that is to say, when the senses move among sense objects freed from attachment and aversion] the heart is purified; when the

1

heart is purified, there is constant and unceasing remembrance of the Self; when there is constant and unceasing remembrance of the Self, all bonds are loosened and freedom is attained."

We next discover the name of Narada mentioned in the Srimad Bhagavatam[1] and there we find him as an illumined soul. Narada requested Vyasa (who was regarded as the compiler of the Vedas, and the author of the Mahabharata) to write the Srimad Bhagavatam. In that connection Narada told Vyasa the history of his life, not only of one birth but of two births.

"Let me tell of my past incarnation, and of how I came to find this divine freedom and peace which I have. My mother was a servant in a retreat where great sages lived. I was reared in close association with them, and I too served them. While I was living in the society of these holy men, my heart was purified."

The grace of a holy man and association with men of God are the chief ways to attain God and divine love. As Swami Vivekananda, a great saint of this modern age, said, "Take refuge in some soul who has already broken his bondage, and in time he will free you through his mercy. Higher still is to take refuge in the Lord, but it is the most difficult; only once in a century can one be found who has really done it." If, however, you are yearning for God with earnestness, you will meet your *guru*. The presence of those who love God makes a place holy, such is the glory of the children of God. They have become united with him, and when they speak, their words are scriptures. The place where they have been becomes filled with holy vibrations, and

---

1 Translated as *The Wisdom of God* by Swami Prabhavananda (G. Putnam & Company, 1943).

those who go there feel them and they also become holy.

Narada continues: "While I was thus living in the society of these holy men, my heart was purified. One day, one of the sages, because of his deep love for me, initiated me into the sacred mysteries of wisdom. The veil of ignorance was removed from me, and I knew my real Self as divine. Then I learned this lesson—that the greatest remedy for all the ills of life, physical or mental, is to surrender the fruits of *karmas* [works] to the Lord. Karma places us in bondage, but by resigning our karma to the Lord we are freed. Work which we perform as service to the Lord creates love and devotion in us. This love and devotion, in turn, bring wisdom; and at last, guided by this wisdom, we surrender ourselves to the Lord of Love and meditate upon him. Thus it is that I attained to wisdom and love."

In the above quotation we find the harmony of all the *yogas*—the paths of union with God through selfless action, devotion, wisdom, and meditation (*karma yoga, bhakti yoga, jnana yoga,* and *raja yoga*). In other words, these four yogas are not separate like airtight compartments. If a man follows one of the yogas with sincerity and earnestness, all the other yogas intermingle in his life.

Narada continues: "I lived with the sages until my mother died, when I left the retreat and wandered about visiting various places. At last I went into a deep forest in search of solitude. Seated under a tree, in a quiet, lonely place, forgetting the world in the love of the Lord, I meditated upon him. Gradually, as my inner vision became clear, I saw the benign Lord of Love seated in the sanctuary of my heart. I was overwhelmed with inexpressible joy, and I could no longer

3

think of myself as separate from God—I had discovered my identity with him. But not for long was I to remain in that state. Again I found myself in the world of the senses; and now, alas, when with all eagerness I sought to reach once more that state of blessedness, it seemed impossible for me to do so. Then I heard a voice from the void. The Lord was speaking as if to console me: 'My child, you will not see me again in this life. Those whose desires are not quenched cannot see me; but because of your devotion to me, I vouchsafed the experience to you once. Saints who are devoted to me gradually give up all desires. Live in the company of the holy, attend upon them, and fix your mind firmly upon me. Thus you will ultimately realize your unity with me. Then will there be no more separation for you, nor will there be for you any more death.'

"In due time I gave up the body and became united with the Lord. I lived in that blessed union for a whole *cycle*. In the beginning of the next cycle I was sent forth into this world where I am now living a life of purity and continence; I can wander about everywhere, in every *loka*, through the grace of the Lord. Wherever I go I play on my *vina* and sing the praises of the Lord, and the Lord of Love is ever manifest in my heart. Those who hear my songs in praise of the Lord find peace and freedom."

Sri Ramakrishna used to say that Narada and Shukadeva are ever-free souls. They are born again and again, for the good of mankind, and are born with the knowledge of God.

In the Srimad Bhagavatam, we find it written that when a sincere yearning for God arises in the heart of a spiritual aspirant, there Narada will appear as the guru. It has already been pointed out that the grace of an illumined soul is necessary to progress in spiritual life. You may read the scriptures and understand them. You may believe in them. But such understanding does not give you religion, does not give you the knowledge of God. It is not scholarly knowledge of the scriptures or theology that makes you spiritual. It is an experience within your own soul, and in order that this experience may unfold in your heart you need the touch of a guru, an illumined soul. To quote Swami Vivekananda: "Divine Incarnations—Jesus, Buddha, Ramakrishna—can give religion. One glance, one touch is enough. That is the power of the Holy Ghost, the 'laying on of hands.' The power was actually transmitted to the disciples by the Master—the 'chain of guru-power.' "

This chain of guru-power continues. Jesus, Buddha, or Ramakrishna are not to be found as gurus at all times. But their power as transmitted to the disciples remains and is handed down from generation to generation. It is transmitted, as it were, in a seed-form to the disciple through the sacred name of God as the Chosen Ideal of the aspirant. As the disciple chants the holy name, as he nourishes the seed, it grows gradually into a tree with flowers and fruit. And, in turn, the disciple becomes the guru. Guru-power is not a power of man, but (in the words of Sri Ramakrishna) "of *Sat-chit-ananda*—God himself."

BEFORE WE UNDERTAKE the study of any subject, we must know our objective in such a study. For instance, if you want to study physics or chemistry or literature or medicine or law, you have an objective. Similarly, when we undertake the study of any scripture, we must have a clear understanding of our objective. And what is that? It is to find the way to God.

God *is*. What is the proof of His existence? It is true that many arguments have been put forward, which seem logical and perhaps scientific, to prove his existence. It is also true that there are scholars and philosophers who deny the existence of God, and their arguments are as logical as those of their opponents. Shankara, one of the seer-philosophers of India, pointed out that supposing the existence of God could be proved through reasoning, no final conclusion could be reached, since you could not gather all the scholars and philosophers past, present, and future, to discuss the question. So where lies the real proof? The real proof is that God can be known and realized. As Shankara pointed out, scriptures alone are not the authority for the existence of God; for along with the study of scriptures, "one must have a personal experience" of the truth of God.

Swami Vivekananda said: "Obey the scriptures until you are strong enough to do without them; then go beyond them. Books are not final. Verification is the only proof of religious truth. Each must verify for himself; and no teacher who says, 'I have seen, but *you* cannot' is to be trusted—only that one who says, 'You can see, too.' All scriptures and all truths, of all times and of all countries, are Vedas because these truths are to be *seen* and anyone may discover them." In that sense alone the Hindus believe that the Vedas are beginningless and endless.

Thus if you merely study the scriptures and do not attempt to verify the truths of the scriptures in your own life, your study is worthless. One who is only

6

versed in the scriptures and has not verified their truths in his personal life is likened by Mohammed to an ass carrying a load of books.

Now, of course, nobody has seen God with these eyes, nobody has heard the voice of God with these ears; yet He can be seen, and one can hear Him speak, and ultimately one can reach union with Him. In the Bhagavad-Gita, Sri Krishna says to his disciple and friend Arjuna, "You cannot see me thus [Krishna's real being in his universal form] with those human eyes. Therefore I give you divine sight." And these are the words of the Psalmist, "Lord, open Thou mine eyes that I may behold wondrous things out of Thy law." From a philosophical standpoint, this opening of the divine sight is known as *Turiya*, "the Fourth," that is to say, a transcendence of the three familiar states of consciousness—waking, dreaming, and dreamless sleep. The capacity to unfold that transcendental knowledge is in every one of us. But in order that our divine sight may be opened, and we may be born in Spirit, we need the grace of a guru, the touch of an illumined soul who shows us the way; and we need to have faith in his words and in the words of the scriptures. Jesus declares, "Verily, verily I say unto thee, Except a man be born of water and of the Spirit, he cannot enter into the Kingdom of God." Initiation by the guru is the same as baptism—"being born of water" in the words of Jesus. And to be born of the Spirit is to attain divine sight. Then as a man struggles to follow the way as taught by the guru he will ultimately realize that it is not by his struggle, but by the grace of God, that he attains His vision or union with Him. This is indeed a gift of God.

Next arises the question: Why does one need God-vision? The answer is already given in the teachings of Sanatkumar to Narada which I have quoted previously: "The Infinite is the source of joy. There is no joy in the finite."

I

SUPREME LOVE DEFINED

NARADA, in the following aphorisms, harmonizes the yoga of divine love with the other yogas—*karma*, the path of selfless service, making all works an offering to God; *jnana*, the path of knowledge or discrimination; and *raja*, the path of meditation.

1. *Now, therefore, we shall teach bhakti, or the religion of divine love.*

This use of the word *now* implies that those who are about to be taught have already gone through a period of spiritual training which has prepared them to be able to understand the true nature of divine love.

The chief qualification is that you must be a spiritual aspirant; in other words, you have to want to know about this subject. If a man is not interested in realizing God, you may lecture to him a hundred times; but it does no good. "You cannot," as Sri Ramakrishna says, "make any dent with nails on a rock, howsoever you hammer on it. The nail will break. Similarly, there is no use in trying to teach a man about God if he is steeped in worldliness."

Everybody does not feel the need for God. Many are satisfied with what the world of mind and senses can offer them. But there comes a time when, through the process of growth and evolution, and also through frustrations in life, a man feels the need for God.

9

SUPREME LOVE DEFINED

In the Bhagavad-Gita, Sri Krishna points out that there are four kinds of men who worship God: One is he who is distressed and world-weary. When he fails to find a way out of his suffering, he prays intensely to God and devotes himself to Him.

There is another kind, who has unfulfilled desires. When he does not find any other way left to him to at-. tain his desires, he worships God and devotes himself to Him.

Then there is another kind, who is the seeker for knowledge. He inquires if this appearance of the world is real or if there is anything beyond it.

Lastly is the man of spiritual discrimination, who realizes that "all is vanity, except to love God." He knows in his heart of hearts that God alone is real, and to him seem "stale, flat, and unprofitable all the uses of this world."

Sri Krishna says that this is the kind of man:

> I see as my very Self.
> For he alone loves me
> Because I am myself:
> The last and only goal
> Of his devoted heart.

But Sri Krishna speaks of all four kinds of men as "noble" indeed.

The fact is, no matter with what motive you begin to worship God and devote yourself to him, you begin to taste the joy in his worship, and all other desires then leave you.

This is illustrated in the Srimad Bhagavatam by the life story of a young boy, Dhruba. He was born a prince, but through circumstances beyond his control, he had to live with his mother in poverty and misery. He realized that only God could help him and his mother to be reestablished in the kingdom, of which he would eventually become ruler. So he went into a deep forest and began to pray to God with great sincerity and earnestness. Narada felt that the young boy was a spiritual aspirant; so he appeared before him and taught him the mysteries of spiritual life. As the boy practiced the disciplines given him, he had the vision of God. Now, as the story goes, God appeared before him in the form of his Chosen Ideal, and said to him: "The king, your father, wants you and your mother back. And he will offer the crown to you."

But Dhruba said, "What need have I of a kingdom, as long as I have you?"

"No," the Lord said, "you desired to be a king, and you must be a king. That is my boon to you." Eventually Dhruba devoted himself entirely to God.

In following the path of divine love, therefore, the one and only qualification is to feel the need for God and to want to devote oneself to him. In this respect, it is unlike any other path. For instance, in order to follow the path of knowledge, "he alone may be considered qualified to seek Brahman who has discrimination, whose mind is turned away from enjoyments, who possesses tranquillity and the kindred virtues, and who feels a longing for liberation" (Shankara). "The *bhakta* [devotee]," on the other hand, in the words of Vivekananda, "has not to suppress any single one of his emotions; he only strives to intensify them and direct them to God."

In the Srimad Bhagavatam we read that Sri Krishna

says to his disciple Uddhava, "Even though not yet
master of his senses, my devotee is never completely
overcome by them; his devotion to me is his particular
and saving grace."

Sri Krishna, in the Bhagavad-Gita, tells his disciple
and friend Arjuna:

> Though a man be soiled
> With the sins of a lifetime,
> Let him but love me,
> Rightly resolved,
> In utter devotion:
> I see no sinner,
> That man is holy.
> Holiness soon
> Shall refashion his nature
> To peace eternal;
> O Son of Kunti,
> Of this be certain:
> The man that loves me,
> He shall not perish.

Once Sri Ramakrishna told his intimate disciples,
"He who seeks earnestly to find God will surely find
him. Know this for certain."

. . . therefore, we shall teach bhakti, or the religion
of divine love.

What is the significance of the word, therefore?
What prompted the saintly author Narada to expound
his gospel of divine love?

He did so because, if a man attains love for God, this
love leads him directly to realize God, experience his
oneness with the Lord, the Self in all beings; and this is

the most natural and easy path. For everyone has love in his heart, only this love has to be directed toward God.

2. *Bhakti is intense love for God.*

Narada does not use the word *God*, but the indefinite neuter pronoun "this"—and in translating the aphorism into English, I have altered it, because "intense love for this," would not convey the intended meaning.

It is interesting to consider why Narada used the pronoun "this," instead of God, or Brahman, or Atman, or Rama, or Krishna, or some other divine name.

One reason is that he wished his teachings to be completely nonsectarian. The use of the pronoun "this" in contrast to "that" suggests that the Reality, no matter by what name it may be called, is nearer than the nearest—the innermost Self of our being; and is to be found within the sanctuary of our own hearts and in the hearts of all beings.

As already stated, God, the ultimate Reality, is to be experienced with the opening of divine sight. Narada avoids defining God anywhere in this treatise, because to define is to limit God. Furthermore, when a man experiences God, he is unable to express Him in terms of relative experiences. To quote the words of Sri Ramakrishna: "When one attains *samadhi*, then alone comes the knowledge of Brahman. In that realization all thoughts cease, one becomes perfectly silent. There is no power of speech left by which to express Brahman."

But again we find that the great sages and seers have tried to express the truth of God in varied ways. Some say he is personal, and others impersonal. Some say

13

he is with form and others without form. Some say he is endowed with divine attributes, others say he is attributeless.

Sri Ramakrishna, in the light of his own mystic experiences, resolved, in his simple way, all such contradictions. "Infinite is God and infinite are his expressions. He who lives continuously in the consciousness of God, and in this alone, knows him in his true being. He knows him as impersonal no less than as personal.

"Brahman, absolute existence, knowledge, and bliss, may be compared to an ocean, without beginning or end. As through intense cold some portions of the water of the ocean freeze into ice, and the formless water appears to have form, so through the intense love of the devotee the formless, infinite Existence manifests himself before him as having form and personality. But forms and aspects disappear before the man who reaches the highest samadhi, who attains the height of nondualistic philosophy, the Vedanta.

"So long as there is still a little ego left, the consciousness that 'I am a devotee,' God is comprehended as personal, and his form is realized. This consciousness of a separate ego is a barrier that keeps one at a distance from the highest realization. The forms of Kali or Krishna are represented as of a dark blue color. Why? Because the devotee has not yet approached them. At a distance the water of a lake appears blue, but when you come nearer, you find it has no color. In the same way, to him who attains the highest truth and experience, Brahman is absolute and impersonal. His real nature cannot be defined in words."

The various ideals of God which devotees worship according to their spiritual tendencies or inclinations may be the Personal God with attributes, under the aspects of Vishnu, Shiva, Kali, Jehovah, Allah and so forth, or incarnations of God, such as Rama, Krishna, Buddha, Christ, or Ramakrishna.

Narada defines bhakti as "intense love" for God. This intense love that the sage speaks of refers to the love that arises in the heart of a devotee who has the vision of God, when he has become intoxicated with divine love. That such love is the same as experiencing God-consciousness is evident also from Narada's descriptions of the nature of this love in the aphorisms which follow.

One day, while Swami Vivekananda was holding classes for a few intimate disciples at Thousand Island Park, he took up the study of Narada's Bhakti Sutras. As Swamiji translated this particular aphorism, he commented upon it by quoting the following words of his master, Sri Ramakrishna: "This world is a huge lunatic asylum where all men are mad—some after money, some after women, some after name or fame, and a few after God. God is the philosopher's stone that turns us to gold in an instant: the form remains, but the nature is changed; the human form remains, but no more can we do harm or commit any sin.

"Thinking of God, some weep, some sing, some dance, some say wonderful things—but all speak of nothing but God."

This all-consuming love arises only when we feel His love for us; this is tangibly felt when we experience ecstasy in God-vision.

My master, Swami Brahmananda, once told me, "Our love is so deep that we do not let you know how

15

much we love you." Indeed this is the same kind of deep love that God has for us—for all beings. And in order that we may feel that love of his by going into ecstasy, we need to practice spiritual disciplines, ". . . to know the love of Christ, which passeth knowledge, that ye might be filled with all the fulness of God." (Eph. 3:19).

Bhakti is of two kinds: *gauni* bhakti refers to the *path* of devotion, the ways and means which lead to the experience of *para bhakti,* intense love for God.

Narada in some of the later aphorisms explains the path of devotion, the ways and means—the particular devotional exercises which the aspirant must practice.

As we follow these spiritual disciplines, first there comes the real conviction that God *is.* In other words, his presence is tangibly felt. We do not have his vision as yet; but a sweetness, a joy, a thrill is felt within. And we become convinced that he knows our innermost thoughts. Next, as we continue in our practice of the presence of God, the vision opens up, through his grace; as we read in the Katha Upanishad: "To the man who has felt him as truly existing he reveals his innermost nature." Simultaneously his love becomes known to a certain extent, and we realize him as our one and only "Beloved." But "intense love," according to Narada, is more than having a vision of God in ecstasy.

Before, however, I try to explain what is meant by this intense love, let me point out that a bhakta, following the path of devotion, begins by worshiping God as a Personal Being, such as Vishnu, Shiva, Kali, and so forth.

Perhaps for the Western devotee it will be easier to

understand the worship of an *avatar*, or divine incarnation, such as Christ, Buddha, or Ramakrishna.

Of course, according to Vedantic tradition, there is not only one avatar. The one God incarnates himself in different ages under different forms and names. In the Bhagavad-Gita, Sri Krishna says:

> When goodness grows weak,
> When evil increases,
> I make myself a body.
> In every age I come back
> To deliver the holy,
> To destroy the sin of the sinner,
> To establish righteousness.

Swami Vivekananda explains why divine incarnations are to be worshiped and meditated upon: "God is both the subject and the object. He is the 'I' and the 'you.' How is this? How to know the knower? The knower cannot know himself; I see everything, but cannot see myself. The Atman, the knower, the Lord of all, the real being, is the cause of all the vision that is in the universe, but it is impossible for him to see himself or know himself, excepting through reflection. You cannot see your own face except in a mirror, and so the Atman, the Self, cannot see its own nature until it is reflected, and this whole universe, therefore, is the Self trying to realize Itself. This reflection is thrown back first from the protoplasm, then from plants and animals and so on from better reflectors, until the best reflector —the perfect man—is reached. If a man who wants to see his face looks in a little pool of muddy water, he will see only an outline. If he comes to a pool of clear

17

water he will see a better image. But only if he looks into a looking glass will he see himself reflected as he really is. The perfect man (the avatar) is the clearest reflection of that being who is both subject and object. You now find why *perfect* men instinctively are worshipped as God in every country. They are the most perfect manifestations of the eternal Self. That is why men worship incarnations such as Christ or Buddha."

Now, let me explain that there are two stages of spiritual experience. The devotee first experiences what is known as *savikalpa samadhi*, that is to say, he has the vision of his Chosen Ideal or particular aspect of God, accompanied by inexpressible bliss. There is still a sense of separateness from God. But at an even higher stage, love, lover, and the Beloved become one; there is complete union with God in this samadhi, which is known as *nirvikalpa*. Then God is experienced as impersonal, immanent, and transcendent. Intense love, prema, refers to this experience.

Sri Ramakrishna defines prema as "the intense love for God that makes one forget the world and forget even his own body—that is, rise above physical consciousness."

This intense love is a transcendental experience of inexpressible bliss in which the ego is completely lost.

Before I give some illustrations from the saints and seers who attained complete union with the Lord, realizing him to be the Self, the true Being within themselves, let me describe the main characteristics of divine love:

First, a true devotee loves the Lord for love's sake. There is no bargaining or shopkeeping in his love. He

18

does not even seek liberation, though, in spite of himself, he becomes liberated.

Another characteristic of divine love is that it knows no fear. Swami Vivekananda said that to worship God through fear of punishment, because of human weaknesses, is degrading religion. Sri Sarada Devi, spiritual consort of Sri Ramakrishna, once said: If a baby plays in mud puddles and gets itself dirty, does the mother throw away the baby? Or does she pick him up, wash him, and then take him on her lap? God is more than our own father or mother. He, alone, is love itself. Swami Brahmananda once told me, "Is there any sin in God's eye? A glance from him burns away all sins like a match put to a heap of cotton."

Lastly, this love knows no rival. To a devotee, God is the one and only Beloved. Sri Chaitanya says in his prayer to the Lord:

O Thou, who stealest the hearts of Thy devotees,
Do with me what Thou wilt—
For Thou art my heart's Beloved, Thou and
Thou alone.

Now let me first give examples from the sages and saints in religions other than that of the Hindus who also realized complete union through love.

Al Hallaj, a Sufi, having experienced the ultimate Truth, declared, "I am the Truth, I am He whom I love, and He whom I love is I."

Mohammed's words, *"Inni — an Allahu la illaha Ana"* is an exact translation of Isaiah: "Verily, I, even I, am God, and there is none else."

Saint Paul says, *"Optimum esse unire deo"*—the best is to be one with God.

19

Dionysius, "It is the nature of love to change a man into that which he loves."

The German mystic Meister Eckhart, "The soul in her hot pursuit of God becomes absorbed in Him and she herself is reduced to naught just as the sun will swallow up and put out dawn. . . . Some there are so simple as to think of God as if he dwelt there and of themselves as being here. It is not so. God and I are one."

Sri Ramakrishna describes the highest vision of God in the following words: "He indeed has attained the supreme illumination who not only realizes the presence of God, but knows him as both personal and impersonal, who loves him intensely, talks to him, partakes of his bliss. Such an illumined soul realizes the bliss of God while he is absorbed in meditation, attaining oneness with the indivisible, Impersonal Being, and he realizes the same bliss when he comes back to normal consciousness and sees this universe as a manifestation of that Being and as a divine play."

In the words of Sri Krishna in the Bhagavad-Gita:

> His heart is with Brahman,
> His eye in all things
> Sees only Brahman
> Equally present,
> Knows his own Atman
> In every creature,
> And all creation
> Within that Atman.

Sri Chaitanya was a great lover of God. Sri Ramakrishna expressed his appreciation of the spiritual greatness of Sri Chaitanya by saying, "Sri Chaitanya used to experience three moods. In the inmost mood he would be absorbed in samadhi, unconscious of the outer world. In the semiconscious mood he would dance in ecstasy but could not talk. In the conscious mood he would sing the glories of God."

In the Srimad Bhagavatam we read how Prahlada, the great devotee of Sri Krishna, when absorbed completely in the consciousness of Brahman, found neither the universe nor its cause; all was to him one Infinite, undifferentiated by name and form. But as soon as he regained the sense of individuality, there was the universe before him, and with it the Lord of the universe—the repository of an infinite number of blessed qualities. So it was with the *gopis*, the shepherdesses of Brindavan. As soon as they lost themselves in their absorbing love for Krishna, they realized their union with him and became Krishnas. But when they knew they were shepherdesses, they looked upon Krishna as one to be worshiped, and immediately "unto them appeared Krishna with a smile on his lotus face, clad in yellow robes, and adorned with garlands, the embodied God of love."

In the life of Sri Ramakrishna we find how, many times during the day, he would become absorbed in God. Then he would realize the unitary consciousness; and later, as he came back to the normal consciousness, he would speak of God as the blissful Mother.

3. *In its intrinsic nature this divine love is immortal bliss.*

What is the true nature of this immortal bliss? It is a state of absolute felicity and beatitude. My master

21

once told me, "People talk of enjoying life; but what do those who are steeped in worldliness and passions know of the joy of life? They alone who devote them-selves to God and find sweetness in him begin to taste the true joy of life." There is a word in Sanskrit, *Ma-dhava*, the Sweet One, which is one of the names of the Lord.

In the Taittiriya Upanishad we read, "The Self-Existent is the essence of felicity. Who could live, who could breathe, if that blissful Self dwelt not within the lotus of the heart? He it is that gives joy." We find in the Svetasvatara Upanishad: "As a soiled piece of metal, when it has been cleaned, shines brightly, so the dweller in the body, when he has realized the truth of the Self, is freed from sorrow and attains to bliss."

A similar truth is to be discovered in the Bible: "Therefore the redeemed of the Lord shall return, and come with singing unto Zion; and everlasting joy shall be upon their head: they shall obtain gladness and joy; and sorrow and mourning shall flee away." (Isa. 51:11)

Says Jesus: "Enter thou into the joy of thy lord." (Matt. 25:21).

Sri Ramakrishna described God as the "Sea of Bliss." Once he asked his young disciple Naren (later known as Swami Vivekananda), "Suppose there is the Sea of Bliss, wouldn't you like to dive into it?"

Naren replied, "Oh, no, I would not like to dive into it, for I might drown; I would rather sit on the bank and sip the nectar."

At this Sri Ramakrishna smiled and said, "No, no, you cannot drown in it, for it is the Sea of Immortality. By diving into it one attains immortality."

This is immortal bliss, in the sense that it never ends. One lives merged in this bliss forever and ever. To attain God is to attain this bliss.

Any happiness or pleasure that a man may derive from obtaining the objects of his desire in the world of the senses is the effect of some cause, and as such is ephemeral and finite. It is true that a man has to undergo spiritual disciplines and make efforts to find God. But these disciplines and efforts are undertaken in order to feel the divine grace; and when that grace is felt, then a man knows that his own efforts would have been impossible without the grace of the Lord.

My master often said, "God is not a commodity that you can buy. It is only through His grace that man finds the bliss of attainment of God."

4. *By attaining It, a man becomes perfect, immortal, and satisfied forever.*

The Sanskrit word *siddha*, which I have translated as becoming *perfect*, also means one who has occult powers. But this meaning is not applicable here. For a devotee or any true spiritual aspirant knows that though occult powers may come to him, even unsought, he must reject them, knowing them to be obstacles to spiritual growth and attainment. We find that the great *yogi* Patanjali, the father of Indian Yoga philosophy, after he has dealt with the many occult powers that can be obtained by following certain practices of concentration, ends by emphatically pointing out that "these are powers in the worldly sense, but the greatest power is to overcome them." They are so many temptations to lure the spiritual aspirant away from the path of God.

The real meaning, therefore, is that when intense love for God arises in the heart of a man he becomes perfect. To attain perfection means to realize oneness with God, or to unfold the divinity which is already within man. As we read in the sayings of Jesus, "Be ye therefore perfect, even as your Father which is in heaven is perfect." The heaven referred to by Christ, we should always remember, is *within*.

Strictly speaking, this perfection is not something to be attained, for the true Being, the Self, the Atman, is one with Brahman. Only ignorance covers the truth of God within us and obstructs our divine sight. Ignorance is the sense of ego, which arises through the identification of the Self with the non-Self—that is to say, by identifying oneself with the mind, senses, and body. When the ego is dissolved, the indwelling God, the Beloved, is realized as our very Self, just as through intense love, lover and Beloved become one.

This perfection is also *moksha* or liberation—which means that when the bonds of ignorance have been cut asunder, a man not only attains freedom from all imperfections and limitations but also from the law of karma and from birth, death, and rebirth. The law of karma, simply stated, means the law of cause and effect. This law of causation works not only in the physical world but also in the moral and mental worlds. "Whatsoever a man soweth, that shall he also reap." This is the law. Our enjoyments or sufferings are the effects of our own karmas. Furthermore, the law of karma is closely connected with the law of reincarnation. Why is one born rich, another poor; one with great intellectual abilities, another dull; one with a

24

beautifully formed body, another lame or blind? If this had been our first birth, then the Creator would be responsible for the differences in mankind. According to some Western philosophers, every child is born with a fund of knowledge, not with a blank mind. This knowledge they ascribe to heredity. But in India it is believed to be made up of impressions obtained in previous lives. Thus all are bound by this law of karma and reincarnation, as long as they identify themselves with the false self—that is, the sense of ego. But when a man realizes his Atman, his true Self, he becomes freed from the law of karma and reincarnation. This is technically known as moksha or liberation.

We read in the Upanishads that for a man who has the knowledge of his true Self, "the knot of ignorance in his heart is loosed, all doubts cease to exist, the effects of all deeds are exhausted." Such a man is known as *jivanmukta*—"free while living on earth." In reality, the true Self is unborn and undying. The following passages from the Katha Upanishad explain this idea:

"The Self is the omniscient Lord. He is not born. He does not die. He is neither cause nor effect. This ancient One is unborn, eternal, imperishable; though the body may be destroyed, he is not killed. If the slayer think that he slays, if the slain think that he is slain, neither of them knows the truth. The Self slays not, nor is he slain. . . . Soundless, formless, intangible, undying, tasteless, odourless, eternal, without beginning, without end, immutable, beyond nature, is the Self. Knowing him as such, one is freed from death. Smaller than the smallest, greater than the greatest, this Self forever dwells within the hearts of all. When a man is free from desire, his mind and senses purified, he beholds the glory of the Self and is without sorrow."

Swami Vivekananda expresses this idea as follows:

"As a man having a book in his hands reads one page and turns it over, goes to the next page, reads that, turns it over, and so on, yet it is the book that is being turned over, the pages that are revolving, and not he— he is where he is always—even so with regard to the soul. The whole of nature is that book which the soul is reading. Each life, as it were, is one page of that book; and that read, it is turned over, and so on and on, until the whole of the book is finished, and the soul becomes perfect, having got all the experiences of nature. Yet at the same time it never moved, nor came nor went; it was only gathering experiences. But it appears to us that we are moving. The earth is moving, yet we think that the sun is moving instead of the earth, which we know to be a mistake, a delusion of the senses. So is all this delusion that we are born and that we die, that we come or that we go. We neither come nor go, nor have we been born. For where is the soul to go? There is no place for it to go. Where is it not already?"

Sri Ramakrishna used to make a pun on the word siddha, which I have translated as "becoming perfect, and free while living." In Bengali it also has another meaning, "becoming boiled." So Sri Ramakrishna used to say, "When a man becomes a siddha [attains perfection and liberation], he becomes soft and tender like boiled potatoes or vegetables"; that is to say, his heart melts in sympathy for his fellow beings and becomes compassionate.

Attaining which he also becomes *immortal* (*amrito bhavati* in the text).

What exactly is meant by immortality? There exists

a general misconception that immortality or eternal life is a continuation of life in time and space. Modern science proves conclusively the impossibility of complete annihilation. The very fact that a being or a thing exists implies a continuity of existence, though the existence may be in a different form and under different conditions. Attaining immortality through the knowledge of the Self or the indwelling God does not mean continuity of existence within time and space. It means realization that the Self is undying, and is beyond time and space. Similar doctrines held by all the other great religions teach, primarily, the life of realization and perfection while one still lives in the world. For instance, what did Christ mean when he told his followers to come unto him that in him they might find eternal life? To come unto Christ or Brahman is nothing but the coming into one's own divine Self, and this Self is beyond time, which, with space and a thousand other conditions of human life, belongs only to the finite world and to those who are still not awakened to the higher Self.

By attaining It, a man becomes . . . satisfied forever.

Perhaps the best commentary on this point is to quote the words of Christ to the woman of Samaria who came to draw water from Jacob's well:

"Whosoever drinketh of this water shall thirst again; but whosoever drinketh of the water that I shall give him shall never thirst; but the water that I shall give him shall be in him a well of water springing up into everlasting life."

5. *On attaining That a man does not desire anything else; he grieves no more, is free from hatred or*

*jealousy; he does not take pleasure in the vanities
of life; and he loses all eagerness to gain anything
for himself.*

As a parallel to this aphorism of Narada, let me
quote Sri Krishna, in the Bhagavad-Gita, explaining
the characteristics of an illumined soul:

> He knows bliss in the Atman
> And wants nothing else.
> Cravings torment the heart:
> He renounces cravings.
> I call him illumined.
>
> Not shaken by adversity,
> Not hankering after happiness;
> Free from fear, free from anger,
> Free from the things of desire.
> I call him a seer, and illumined.
>
> The bonds of his flesh are broken.
> He is lucky, and does not rejoice:
> He is unlucky, and does not weep.
> I call him illumined.

Now let us examine the meaning of each of the parts
of this aphorism:

*On attaining That a man does not desire anything
else;*

Shankara says: "The fruit of illumination is the
stilling of desire; the fruit of stilled desire is experience
of the bliss of the Atman, whence follows peace."

Desire arises from a sense of limitation and imper-
fection. A man of attainment feels no lack; what else is

28

there for him to desire? There are two words in Sanskrit—*nishkama*, which means desirelessness, and *purnakama*, which means *complete fulfillment of all desires*. A man of God is purnakama, because in him
there is a complete fulfillment. There is nothing more
to gain or to achieve. It is said in the Bhagavad-Gita:
"Then he knows that infinite happiness which can be
realized by the purified heart but is beyond the grasp
of the senses. He stands firm in that realization. Because of it, he can never again wander from the inmost
truth of his being." And later:

> Now that he holds it
> He knows this treasure
> Above all others.

There is a difference between a spiritual aspirant
and a man of attainment. To quote the Bhagavad-Gita
again:

> The abstinent run away from what they desire
> But carry their desires with them;
> When a man enters Reality,
> He leaves his desires behind him.

But there is one desire left in him. And that is to
serve God in mankind. The heart of an illumined soul
moves in sympathy with the sufferings of others. His
heart becomes full of compassion.

When Sri Ramakrishna asked Naren what he would
like most, Naren replied that he would like to remain
absorbed in samadhi, coming back only occasionally to
normal consciousness in order to sustain his body by

eating and drinking, and then again becoming absorbed in samadhi. To this Sri Ramakrishna said, "Shame on you! I thought you were greater than that." Then Sri Ramakrishna reminded him of the ideal of service to God through mankind—not merely to taste the bliss of God for one's own self, but to help others to taste of the same bliss.

Truly has it been said in the Bhagavad-Gita:

> Who burns with the bliss
> And suffers the sorrow
> Of every creature
> Within his own heart,
> Making his own
> Each bliss and each sorrow:
> Him I hold highest
> Of all the yogis.

... he grieves no more,
Only "he suffers the sorrow of every creature."
He ... is free from hatred and jealousy;
Jealousy or hatred arise from unfulfilled desire. How could jealousy or hatred exist in a man who sees his Beloved everywhere?

But supposing someone hurts or insults a holy man. How would he react? The best illustration of that is given in the "Song of the Mendicant" in the Srimad Bhagavatam. The mendicant was badly hurt and insulted by some ignorant people. And he walked on, saying to himself, "Even if thou dost think another person is causing thee happiness or misery, thou art really neither happy nor wretched, for thou art the Atman, the changeless Spirit; thy sense of happiness and misery is due to a false identification of thy Self with the body, which alone is subject to change. Thy Self is the real Self in all. With whom shouldst thou be angry for causing pain if accidentally thou dost bite thy tongue with thy teeth?"

. . . *he does not take pleasure in the vanities of life;*

His heart is in Brahman, the eternal treasure, in whom is the abiding bliss. So naturally he cannot give his heart to pleasures that are only fleeting.

As Plotinus says: "There are no more two, but one; the soul is no more conscious of the body and mind, but knows that she has what she desired, and that she is where no deception can come, and she would not exchange that bliss for all the heaven of heavens."

. . . *and he loses all eagerness to gain anything for himself.*

This does not mean however that he becomes inert and does not act. It is true that as Sri Krishna says in the Bhagavad-Gita: "When a man has found delight and satisfaction and peace in the Atman, then he is no longer obliged to perform any kind of action. He has nothing to gain in the world by action, and nothing to lose by refraining from action." However, Sri Krishna urges his disciple to act, saying, "Your motive in working should be to set others, by your example, on the path of duty."

Sri Krishna continues:

> The ignorant work
> For the fruit of their action:
> The wise must work also
> Without desire

31

Pointing man's feet
To the path of duty.

Let them show by example
How work is holy
When the heart of the worker
Is fixed on the Highest.

There is another meaning of the last sentence in this aphorism: he does not exert himself. That is to say, he does not act by his own will. He has completely surrendered his will to the will of the Lord. As Tennyson said:

Our wills are ours, we know not how,
Our wills are ours to make them thine.

A conversation I once had with my master, Swami Brahmananda, illustrates how an illumined soul acts as directed by the will of the Lord. One day he asked me to look in the almanac to find an auspicious date for his departure from Madras. As I did so, I could not help smiling. Maharaj[1] noticed this and asked me why I was amused. I replied, "Well, Maharaj, you always go through this routine whenever you plan to go anywhere, but then you suddenly make up your mind to leave on some other day."

At this Maharaj said: "Do you think I do anything according to my own will? The devotees insist upon fixing some date for my going, so to avoid constant pestering I fix a tentative date. But I do not move, or do anything until I know the will of the Lord."

1 Swami Brahmananda was more familiarly known as Maharaj.

"Do you mean to say," I asked, "that you are always guided by the will of the Lord?"

"Yes."

"Well, Maharaj, I too may think or feel that I am doing the will of God, when actually I am only following my own inclinations, and attributing them to God's will. Isn't that what you do?"

"No, my son, it is not the same."

"Then do you mean to say that you actually see God and talk to him directly and know his will?"

"Yes, I wait until I know his will directly and he tells me what I should do."

"For everything you do?"

"Yes, for everything I do I have the direct guidance of God."

"And do you accept only those disciples he wants you to accept?"

"Yes."

After this talk with him, I began to better understand his peculiar way of acting. For example, whenever any of us would ask his advice, he would say, "Wait. My brain is not working today," or "My stomach is upset, I'll answer tomorrow." Sometimes many tomorrows would pass before the disciple got any definite answer. But when Maharaj did finally speak there was always a special power behind his words.

6. *The devotee may first become intoxicated with bliss. Then, having realized That, he becomes inert and silent and takes his delight in the Atman.*

Before I explain the aphorism, let me point out that there is no uniform standard of external conduct or behavior that can be applied to a perfect man. Generally, people judge a holy man by their own standard of how they think he should act and behave. A holy man is bound by no conventions. But the inner experience of all illumined souls, at the highest level of consciousness, is one and the same—be they Hindus, Christians, Moslems, or Jews. They all have the inner experience of bliss and sweetness. Externally, however, they may appear like ordinary men attending to their daily duties.

Sri Ramakrishna described a perfect soul in the following ways: Sometimes he will act like a five-year-old child, or he may seem intoxicated, or mad. Or he may be apparently inert—silent and motionless. He is not bound by any law or code—but nothing he does will be immoral and unethical. His actions and motives are selfless without his trying to be selfless, just as a flower emits its fragrance.

I have also seen how illumined souls may seem "harder than thunder," though in their inner nature they are "tenderer than petals of a flower." My own master would sometimes scold me vehemently. Yet I always knew in my heart of hearts that he was correcting me because he loved me. He said to me one day: "The mother holds the baby on her lap and spanks it; and the baby cries 'Mother, mother.'"

He . . . *becomes intoxicated* . . . There is a line in a song by Ramprasad, a devotee of Divine Mother: "My mind is intoxicated because I have drunk of the nectar at the blessed feet of Mother, but to drunkards I seem to be a drunkard."

In the Chhandogya Upanishad we find a passage which symbolically expresses the idea of spiritual drunkenness in the following way: "In the world of Brahman there is a lake whose waters are like nectar, and whosoever tastes thereof is straightway drunk with joy; and beside that lake is a tree which yields the juice of immortality."

Swami Shivananda, a disciple of Sri Ramakrishna, told us one day, "Get up early in the morning and meditate and perform *japa* to your heart's content. That will keep your mind on a higher level. I myself do that. I meditate in the morning, and the whole day passes, as it were, in intoxication."

Let me quote in this connection the description given by a disciple of Swami Brahmananda of the divine inebriation he experienced while he was visiting the temple of Jagannath at Puri. He has always felt that such an experience was possible to him only through the grace of his *guru* and through the grace of the Lord.

These are his own words: "I went on a pilgrimage to the temple of Jagannath with a brother-disciple of mine. One of the priests was our guide. In order to enter the innermost shrine, one has to go by a passage to the left of the shrine inside the huge temple. As we were about to enter this passage, I suddenly heard a sound like that of thunder coming to strike me. (I must admit here that I was not approaching the shrine with any special reverence or devotion; indeed, I was rather dry in my heart.) For a moment, as the "thunder" actually struck me, I was terrified. But I had no time to go on being afraid, for I lost consciousness. I faintly heard my brother-disciple asking the priest to take hold of my left arm; he himself was already holding my right arm. After they had taken my arms, I was not conscious that anyone was supporting me. I must have had a little consciousness left in me, though I was not aware who I was or where I was. I felt intoxicated, as

35

if I had drunk bottles of wine, and I remember I was dragging my feet. Then as I came nearer to the sanctum sanctorum, there arose within me, in English, the word *God, God, God,* although my mother tongue is Bengali. Then a thrill passed through my whole being. And as I entered into the inner shrine, I became completely unconscious of the external world. All I had was an awareness that I was experiencing a vision which suddenly opened up—I do not know if my eyes were open or closed. I did not see the shrine with walls around me, nor did I see the crowd of pilgrims who must have been there, nor did I see the images of the deities in the shrine. I only saw an ocean of light and waves of bliss striking me, which increased in intensity and beggared all description.

"I do not know how long I was in the shrine. But I do remember that when I was brought out of the shrine and stood in the open courtyard of the temple, I felt that I was being held by my arms. I stood up straight and shook myself free.

"Much later I asked my brother-disciple how he knew that I was about to lose consciousness. He simply replied, 'I lived a long time with Maharaj. That's how I know.' "

Indeed, it is impossible to count the number of times that Maharaj and the other disciples of Sri Ramakrishna became intoxicated with the bliss of God. We ourselves have often seen them immersed in that bliss. As for Sri Ramakrishna, he would become intoxicated even by uttering the name of God in any of his aspects. When he went to the temple of Divine Mother and when he returned he would be so inebriated that a disciple would always be present to hold him. Once, a man who did not know Sri Ramakrishna saw him in that condition and remarked, "That fellow must be blind drunk!"

There is a beautiful description of this state in the Gospel of Sri Ramakrishna:

"Suddenly the Master stood up and went into samadhi, repeating the Mother's name. Coming down a little to the sense plane, he danced and sang:

I drink no ordinary wine, but Wine of Everlasting Bliss,
As I repeat my Mother Kali's name;
It so intoxicates my mind that people take me to be drunk!
First my guru gives me molasses for the making of the Wine;
My longing is the ferment to transform it.
Knowledge, the maker of the Wine, prepares it for me then;
And when it is done, my mind imbibes it from the bottle of the mantra,
Taking the Mother's name to make it pure.
Drink of this Wine, says Ramprasad, and the four fruits of life are yours."[1]

To utter the name of God, in the devotional literature of the Hindus, is described as "to drink the nectar of the name of God."

Similar experiences of intoxication with the bliss of God are to be found in the lives of the mystics of all religions of the world.

---

1 *The Gospel of Sri Ramakrishna*, trans. Swami Nikhilananda (New York: Ramakrishna-Vivekananda Center, 1942), p. 95.

SUPREME LOVE DEFINED

In the Svetasvatara Upanishad we read, "Set fire to the Self within by the practice of meditation. Be drunk with the wine of divine love. Thus shall you reach perfection."

Having realized That . . . I have translated the Sanskrit word *jnatwa* as "having realized" because the Reality—the eternal beloved One—is forever within the shrine of our hearts. He is not obtained from outside ourselves like an object. But the Kingdom of God within becomes revealed.

He may appear . . . *inert or silent* . . . This refers to samadhi, the experience of unitary consciousness which transcends the three ordinary states of consciousness—those of waking, dreaming, and dreamless sleep. Of all the exemplars of our present age, Sri Ramakrishna is the only one who is known to have entered samadhi many times every day. So I shall describe his condition by quoting from M. (who was an eyewitness), in the Gospel of Sri Ramakrishna:

". . . a strange transformation came over Sri Ramakrishna. . . . At the sight of Rakhal,[1] his eyes expressed the utmost tenderness, like the love of Mother Yasoda toward her baby son Krishna. With intense love in his voice, he uttered the holy name, 'Govinda, Govinda,' and went into deep samadhi. The devotees looked at him struck with wonder. His body was motionless, like a statue. His senses and sense organs completely ceased to function. His eyes were fixed on the tip of his nose, and his breathing almost ceased."

Sri Ramakrishna also pointed out in one of his talks

[1] Rakhal later became Swami Brahmananda.

that the sign of a man who has attained the supreme wisdom is that he becomes silent.

Shankara says: "This state of silence is a state of complete peace, in which the intellect ceases to occupy itself with the unreal. In this silence, the great soul who knows and is one with Brahman enjoys unmingled bliss forever."

He . . . *takes his delight in the Atman.* This refers to the man of God who returns to normal consciousness after realizing the truth of Brahman.

In the Vivekachudamani[1] Shankara has beautifully described the condition in which the knower of Brahman lives:

"The ocean of Brahman is full of nectar—the joy of the Atman. The treasure I have found there cannot be described in words. The mind cannot conceive of it. My mind fell like a hailstone into that vast expanse of Brahman's ocean. Touching one drop of it, I melted away and became one with Brahman. And now, though I return to human consciousness, I abide in the joy of the Atman."

---

1 *Shankara's Crest-Jewel of Discrimination,* trans. Swami Prabhavananda and Christopher Isherwood (Vedanta Press, 1947).

II

RENUNCIATION AND SELF-SURRENDER

7. *Bhakti cannot be used to fulfill any desire, being itself the check to all desire.*

In this context, bhakti means supreme and intense love for God. When there arises in the heart of a devotee a maddening love for the enchantingly beloved Lord, he no longer has any desire left in him for the objects or pleasures of this universe. When a man finds God, all his desires become fulfilled in Him. If you live on the bank of a mighty river, whose water is clear and pure, you do not dig a well to satisfy your thirst.

Shankara thus describes the bliss of a God-man: "The ego has disappeared. I have realized my identity with Brahman and so all my desires have melted away. I have risen above my ignorance and my knowledge of this seeming universe. What is this joy that I feel? Who shall measure it? I know nothing but joy, limitless, unbounded."

Here is an incident from the life of Swami Vivekananda, when as a young man he was still known as Naren. It illustrates that bhakti itself is the check to all worldly desires:

"Early in 1884, Naren's father Viswanath died of a heart attack; he had been ailing for some time. . . . When the time came to look into Viswanath's financial affairs, it was found that he had been spending more

40

than he earned and had left nothing but debts. . . . Naren set himself to find employment with renewed energy. He got a post in an attorney's office. He translated some books. But these were temporary jobs; they brought no real security to his mother and brothers. So now Naren decided to ask Ramakrishna to pray on his behalf that the family's money troubles might be overcome. Ramakrishna answered that it was for Naren himself to pray. He must forget his earlier scruples, accept the existence of Divine Mother and pray for her help. 'Today is Tuesday,' Ramakrishna added, 'a day specially sacred to Mother. Go to the temple tonight and pray. Mother will grant you whatever you ask for. I promise you that.'

"At nine o'clock, Ramakrishna sent him to the temple. As Naren was on his way there, a kind of drunkenness possessed him, he was reeling. And when he entered the temple, he saw at once that the Divine Mother was actually alive. Naren was overwhelmed and prostrated himself again and again before her shrine, exclaiming, 'Mother—grant me discrimination, grant me detachment, grant me divine knowledge and devotion, grant me that I may see you without obstruction, always!' His heart was filled with peace. The universe completely disappeared from his consciousness and Mother alone remained.

"When Naren came back from the temple, Ramakrishna asked him if he had prayed for the relief of his family's wants. Naren was taken aback; he had forgotten to do so. Ramakrishna told him to return quickly and make the prayer. Naren obeyed, but again he became drunk with bliss, forgot his intention and prayed only for detachment, devotion and knowledge as before. 'Silly boy!' said Ramakrishna, when he returned and confessed this. 'Couldn't you control yourself a little, and remember that prayer? Go back again and tell Mother what you want—be quick!' This time Naren's experience was different. He did not forget the prayer. But when he came for the third time before the shrine he felt a sense of deep shame; what he had been about to ask seemed miserably trivial and unworthy. 'It was,' he said later, 'like being graciously received by a king and then asking for gourds and pumpkins.' So, once more, he asked only for detachment, devotion and knowledge."[1]

Ramakrishna, however, blessed Naren's family, saying, "They will never lack plain food and clothing."

This is a fact within the experience of any spiritual aspirant; as he comes nearer to God, his heart is so filled with love and devotion that there is no room for any other desire. There is a song of Ramprasad which says that even to gain the position of an Indra, the king of gods, seems as nothing to one on whom the Divine Mother has cast her gracious glance.

8. *Renunciation means dedication of all activities, secular as well as sacred, to God.*

The word renunciation sounds grim; but, in fact, it means renouncing the smaller for the greater, sweetened milk for ice cream; you receive something better in exchange. There is the story of a holy man and a king. The king came to the holy man and said, "You are such a great soul, you have such great renuncia-

---

1 Christopher Isherwood, *Ramakrishna and His Disciples* (New York: Simon and Schuster, 1965).

tion." The holy man replied, "Oh, no, you are the greater man of renunciation. You see, I have renounced the finite, puny, ephemeral things, for that which is infinite and everlasting. But you have renounced the eternal for the noneternals of life. Hence your renunciation is greater than mine."

Sri Ramakrishna used to say that the ideal of renunciation must grow naturally, one must not force oneself to renounce. And he gave this example: If a man tries to remove the scab from a sore before it is completely healed, the sore will get worse. Let the scab dry up, then it will fall away by itself. Similarly, you must move toward God, pray for pure devotion, learn to love God and, as that love grows in your heart, passions will naturally come under control and your heart will cease to be attached to worldliness. Thus, the path of devotion is the most natural and the easiest to follow; because as you think of God more and more, love will grow in your heart, and as love grows, discrimination, dispassion, and purity of heart will come to you naturally.

The analogy given is that God is a big magnet and that our passions and worldly enjoyments are smaller magnets. But when these smaller magnets attract us, we do not feel the pull of the big magnet because of the dirt and dust which have gathered in our minds. However, if we long for God and weep for him, the dirt and dust are washed away, and we feel the attraction of the big magnet—God—as divine grace.

The perfect soul has neither desire nor craving; his renunciation of worldliness has become natural to him. He "lives, moves, and has his being in God," consciously, with full awareness.

RENUNCIATION AND SELF-SURRENDER

Renunciation does not mean shunning all activities, but that all the actions of a man of God, whether secular or spiritual, are dedicated to God. His work becomes worship of God. He may live in the world but is not of it. As Sri Ramakrishna used to say, "Let the boat stay on the water, but let not the water stay in the boat."

It is said in the Bhagavad-Gita:

"Freedom from activity is never achieved by abstaining from action. Nobody can become perfect by merely ceasing to act. In fact, nobody can ever rest from his activity even for a moment. [Here activity means also mental action, conscious or subconscious.] All are helplessly forced to act by the gunas.

"A man who renounces physical actions but still lets his mind dwell on the objects of his sensual desire is deceiving himself. He can only be called a hypocrite. The truly admirable man controls his senses by the power of his will. All his actions are disinterested. All are directed along the path to union with Brahman.

"The world is imprisoned by its own activity, except when actions are performed as worship of God. Therefore you must perform every action sacramentally and be free from all attachment to results."

Sri Krishna teaches the secret of worshiping God through all one's activities. He says:

> Whatever your action,
> Food or worship;
> Whatever the gift you give to another;
> Whatever you vow to the work of the Spirit;
> O Son of Kunti,
> Lay these also as offerings before me.

Shankara, having realized this secret of work, said, "Whatever I do, O Lord, all that is thy worship."

Worldliness means to feel that "I" am the doer, and attachment to worldly objects and persons is to feel that "I" *possess* them, they belong to "me," and they are "mine." Sri Ramakrishna often used to say, "I am the machine, Thou art the operator. I am the house, Thou art the dweller in the house. I do as Thou makest me do, I speak as Thou makest me speak."

God is the king, the ruler within our hearts, but when, through ignorance, we become forgetful of his benign presence within us, we have usurped his throne. We must shun the false sense of ego and let the true king, the Lord within, rule us, guide us in every way. Say day and night, "Not I, not I, but Thou, my Lord."

A perfect soul has freed himself from all sense of false ego and, having completely surrendered himself to God, has achieved his union with him.

The spiritual aspirant should try to imitate the lives and actions of the enlightened ones. He should keep his goal always before him: union with God. The best method of reaching this goal is to cultivate faith that union can be achieved, not in the distant future but at any moment. At the same time, however, he must have patience. Patience and perseverance are the two characteristics of a true spiritual aspirant.

9. *A bhakta's renunciation means that his whole soul goes toward God, and whatever militates against love for God he rejects.*

His whole soul goes toward God.
In other words, he becomes unified with Him in

45

every way. As long as a man lives, he has passions. But a bhakta's passions are sublimated, that is to say, they are directed toward God. There is no repression there.

When the whole soul goes toward God, something more happens. Such a man's life melts in sympathy. God is love. His love is motiveless. As a devotee begins to think of God more and more, and begins to follow the disciplines of spiritual life, he realizes this motiveless and overwhelming love of God toward all beings, in spite of their weaknesses and human failings. By loving God the devotee experiences that same love. He begins to see his Beloved's face everywhere and in every being, and he lives to serve God in all.

We had the blessed fortune to meet the disciples of Sri Ramakrishna, who to us were the embodiments of this divine love. What most attracted us to them was their motiveless love for us. We had nothing to offer them, yet they loved us more than our own parents or friends or any ordinary human being.

Furthermore, a devotee who has whole-souled love for God is freed from egotism; his will has become unified with God's will. Of course, in order to teach mankind, he has to have a sense of ego, but his ego, as Sri Ramakrishna said, is the "ego of knowledge." It does no harm.

Swami Brahmananda once told me that Vivekananda was completely free from any sense of "I" as separate from Brahman. Swami Turiyananda, another disciple of Sri Ramakrishna, said to me, "Whenever Swamiji [Vivekananda] would use the word 'I,' his 'I' was identified with the 'universal I, Brahman.' "

A bhakta's renunciation means that his whole soul

goes toward God, and whatever militates against love for God he rejects. (I repeat the previous aphorism for the convenience of the reader, because it is further explained in the two aphorisms which follow.)

10. *Whole-souled devotion means giving up every other refuge and taking refuge in God.*

Swami Vivekananda once said: "If there were only a few souls who could come out and say, 'I possess nothing but God,' they could change the world."

Man seeks security, but how and where can he find it? Most people, though they may have everything that the world has to offer, still feel insecure. We may think wealth or possessions can give us security, or that name and fame, or objects of pleasure or enjoyment can make us happy and give us security. But ultimately we realize that we are still insecure, and we feel frustrated. The only security is to be found in God, who is the innermost Self of our being. All else will fail us, but the Lord never fails us. We must take refuge in him alone.

When, through spiritual struggles, we become established in constant recollectedness of God, when there arises true love for God in our hearts, then alone we realize that "He is our supreme goal, he is our support, he is our Beloved Lord, he is the witness within us, he is our supreme abode, he is our true refuge, and he is our real friend."

A devotee, whose whole soul goes toward God, knows in his heart of hearts, "My one strength is God, my one treasure is God, my one refuge is God."

Swami Sadananda, a devoted disciple of Swami Vivekananda, took his one and only refuge in Swamiji, for to this disciple, Swamiji, his guru, was God. He was bedridden and could not move without help. There were two young brothers, devoted to him, who were taking the greatest care of him. Once a thought arose in them that the swami was helpless without them to serve him. The swami read their thought and said to them, "Look here, I can't move by myself. But you leave me there on the street. My Swamiji will come and take care of me, and devotedly serve me." This is true faith, and this is what is meant by "God is my one and only refuge."

11. *To reject whatever militates against love for God means performance of such secular and sacred activities as are favorable to devotion to God.*

A true devotee avoids engaging in such activities as would make him forget God. What is good action and what is bad action? What is right, and what is wrong? The one criterion is that that is good and right which helps you to keep your mind in God, which helps you to keep remembrance of God; and evil or wrong is that which makes you forget God, which leads you away from God.

In this connection, let me quote from the Katha Upanishad the teachings of Yama to the young boy Nachiketa on the secret of immortality: "The good is one thing; the pleasant is another. These two, differing in their ends, both prompt to action. Blessed are they that choose the good; they that choose the pleasant miss the goal.

"Both the good and the pleasant present themselves

to men. The wise having examined both, distinguish the one from the other. The wise prefer the good to the pleasant; the foolish, driven by fleshly desires, prefer the pleasant to the good."

12. *Scriptures are to be followed as long as one's spiritual life is not firmly established in God.*

Until a man attains intense love for God he must follow the injunctions of the scriptures, for they are revealed truths and guides to a spiritual aspirant. It has been said that a spiritual aspirant must have *shraddha*, that is, faith in the words of his guru and in the words of the scriptures.

It has also been declared by Sri Krishna in the Bhagavad-Gita: "He who flouts the commandments of the scriptures, and acts on the impulse of his desires, cannot reach perfection, or happiness, or the highest goal.

"Let the scriptures be your guide, therefore, in deciding what you must do, and what you must abstain from. First learn the path of action, as the scriptures teach it. Then act accordingly."

There is a parable of Sri Ramakrishna which shows how one should follow the scriptures until one has achieved the goal: A man received a letter from his family with a list of things he was to buy and bring home with him. He misplaced the list and became worried. After a long search, he found the list; he read it and bought all the things written there. Then he threw away the letter. He did not need it any more. Similarly, the spiritual aspirant must follow the injunctions of the scriptures until he has realized the goal. After that, what need is there of scriptures?

Sri Ramakrishna used to give another example: "You need a fan to fan yourself as long as it is hot. But when the spring breeze blows, you do not need the fan any more."

Sri Krishna says in the Bhagavad-Gita: "When the whole country is flooded, the reservoir becomes superfluous. So to the illumined seer, the Vedas are all superfluous."

13. *Or else there is the risk of falling.*

If a man who has not yet attained God-consciousness and become established in constant recollectedness of God neglects to follow the spiritual disciplines prescribed by the scriptures and his guru, there is always the danger that past impressions of sense pleasures and attachment to worldly objects and persons will arise to threaten him, and that he will then fall from his path to union with God.

14. *Social customs and practices need only be followed until one's love for God grows intense; but acts such as eating, drinking, etc., which are necessary for the preservation of the body, must not be given up.*

Social customs and practices are not specifically enjoined by the scriptures: they are different in different countries and among different races. For instance, people of different countries dress differently. These customs and practices, though merely conventional, are to be followed until intense love for God grows in the heart. Holy Mother has a saying to this effect, that one should act and behave as dictated by the circumstances in which one is placed. And there is the saying of St. Ambrose, "When you are in Rome, live in the Roman style." A man of God may become forgetful of outward forms and cannot be expected to observe them strictly. However, a man of God is not neglectful of natural and biological activities, such as eating, drinking, sleeping, etc., for the preservation of his body, nor does he neglect his health. A man of God considers his mind and body as not belonging to himself, but to God, who is the indwelling Spirit in him.

III

EXEMPLARS OF DIVINE LOVE

15. *The characteristics of divine love have been described variously by sages because of difference in their viewpoints.*

The first few aphorisms which we have already considered have defined the characteristics of supreme love as directed toward God. In the next few aphorisms Narada is quoting the definitions of bhakti, or divine love, as given by other great seers and sages. As we shall see, these definitions of bhakti show the ways and means to attain the supreme love for God. Though these definitions seem to be different, they are not actually so. Narada includes them all in order to give a complete description of the characteristics of divine love, and he ends by harmonizing them all in his own definition.

The highest truth can never be expressed by words. As Sri Ramakrishna said, the supreme truth of God has "never been defiled through the lips of man," that is, has never been expressed in words. He furthermore says, "Even the Vedas and the other scriptures of the world have been defiled, for they have been uttered by the lips of man." The Truth, which is the Truth of all truths, is only to be experienced; and when a man of God experiences that, he becomes full to the brim, as it were. He becomes silent.

Yet we find that the seers and sages, having drunk

deep of that wine of love, try to give utterance to the Truth. And they speak differently. This is because they can only express an aspect of the Truth. It is only relative truth that can be expressed, and never that which is absolute. Even Christ, Buddha, and Ramakrishna can express themselves only from a relative standpoint. Hence, sometimes they may differ in their expressions. They are not contradictory, but supplementary. To give an illustration, suppose you want to take a photograph of the sun. You take a picture from where you stand; then you go nearer to the sun and take a picture from there, and you go nearer and nearer and take pictures from different distances. Then you compare those pictures. They do not appear to be the same. But nevertheless they are true pictures of the same sun. "Truth is one, sages call It variously."

16. *Vyasa, son of Parasara, defines bhakti as devotion to acts of worship and the like.*

Vyasa is well known as the compiler of the Vedas and the Puranas—the revealed and auxiliary scriptures of India.

In his definition of bhakti, he lays stress on worship and such acts as will keep our minds fixed on God.

Worship includes ritual, with the offering of flowers, fruit, water, light, incense, and so forth. It also includes mental worship as well as japa, or chanting the name of the Lord. All these kinds of worship help one to keep the mind fixed on God.

Before I go any further, let me tell what my master taught me in this connection.

Once I was arranging a basket of flowers in Maharaj's room. He entered the room and inquired if I had offered some flowers for worship in the shrine. I answered, "No," and I thought to myself that the shrine merely contained a picture. He seemed to read my thoughts, and asked me, "Do you think there is nothing in the shrine but a picture?" I replied, rather nervously, "Yes." Then he asked me if I had ever done any external ritualistic worship. I said, "No, because I do not believe in it." My master did not try to convince me by argument of the efficacy of ritualistic worship. He simply said, "I am asking you to do it." I replied, "I will obey you." Then, when I started to do the worship, after only three days, I was convinced of the truth as taught in the Bhagavad-Gita:

> Whatever man gives me
> In true devotion:
> Fruit or water,
> A leaf, a flower:
> I will accept it.
> That gift is love,
> His heart's dedication.

I must confess that I offered the worship not with any true devotion, but rather mechanically, yet my guru and the Lord convinced me in their mysterious ways that He accepted what I offered.

However, I must also point out that my master did not ask every one of his disciples to perform the ritual worship. He taught each disciple differently, according to each one's temperament.

Ritualistic worship is a great aid in fixing one's mind and heart in God. If one learns the ritualism of the

Hindus, one can find in it a practical way to learn through devotion to see God or Brahman and Atman or Self as one. There is a saying, "Be a God to worship God." This is the principle underlying the performance of external worship. Most people misunderstand external worship, thinking it to be *dualistic.* In fact, it is *nondualistic,* for the worshiper must not only perform the ritual but try to meditate on his unity with Brahman.

It is true that you offer flowers and other items externally to the picture or image of a deity or an avatar—your Chosen Ideal. But first you meditate on your union with Brahman. Then you meditate on your Chosen Ideal as Atman-Brahman, within the shrine of your own heart. Then you bring forth the Lord from your heart, place him in front of you and think of the picture or the image as alive. Then it is that you offer flowers and other items to the Lord, while thinking that there is the same Lord, the same Brahman, in each of these items. "You worship," as the saying goes, "Mother Ganges with the water of the river, Mother Ganges." Before you finish your worship, you perform a certain number of japa, mentally chanting the *mantra* you received from your guru. According to Hindu tradition, one is not allowed to perform any formal ritualistic worship before being initiated with a mantra by a guru.

There is also a widely accepted but mistaken idea that formal worship is only for the beginners in spiritual life. It is true that it is a great aid to beginners, as I have already stated. But men of God, who have experienced the supreme Truth, oneness with Brahman, often continue to practice ritual worship. Shankara,

Ramanuja, Sri Chaitanya, and Sri Ramakrishna engaged in worship even after realization.

There is an incident in the life of Vivekananda which was described by Swami Bodhananda, one of his disciples, who happened to be present on the occasion. Swamiji was seated in front of the picture of Sri Ramakrishna in the shrine, with a tray of flowers sprinkled with sandal paste. He asked his disciples to meditate with him. Swamiji meditated for a while, then he stood up with the tray of flowers, and worshiped each disciple in turn, placing a flower as an offering on the head of each one. After he had thus worshiped all the disciples, he offered the rest of the flowers to the picture of Sri Ramakrishna.

Worship also includes mental worship. You do not need to gather flowers and all the other paraphernalia for worship. You can mentally offer flowers and all the items you can think of to the Lord.

There is a story of a holy man who used to visit other holy men while they were meditating. Once when the holy man he was visiting came out of his meditation, the visitor told him, "Ah, you were in a store buying shoes for the Lord." The other holy man smiled and replied, "Yes, that is true." There is a very important lesson in this story. If your mind becomes distracted while meditating on the Lord, use such distractions also as aids to think of the Lord, by connecting them with him. There is a saying, "Adopt any means to let your mind dwell in Krishna."

In this aphorism, we find the definition of *bhakti as devotion to acts of worship, and the like.*

And the like refers to service of God in mankind. That also is an act of worship.

17. *The sage Garga defines bhakti as devotion to hearing and praising the name of God.*

Sri Chaitanya wrote a famous hymn to the Lord, from which I quote here a few lines:

> Chant the name of the Lord and His glory
>   unceasingly
> That the mirror of the heart may be
>   wiped clean
> And quenched that mighty forest fire,
> Worldly lust, raging furiously within.

In almost every religion, emphasis has been laid upon singing hymns and praises to God. Ramprasad, a great saint, realized his union with God entirely by singing songs to the Divine Mother, his Chosen Ideal, songs that he had composed himself. His life story is interesting. He was a clerk in an office, and his duty was to keep accounts of income and expenditure in a book. But instead of keeping accounts, the book was filled with songs to the Divine Mother which he had composed during the office hours. One day the owner came to examine his account book. Instead of getting angry with Ramprasad, he was impressed by his genius as a composer of devotional songs, and he said to him, "Look here. You go home. I'll give you your regular salary so that you do not have to work for your living. You compose devotional songs like these and sing them."

This aphorism also refers to study and exposition of the scriptures, discourses on spiritual topics, and the

57

composition of hymns and songs in praise of the Lord. In the Srimad Bhagavatam we read:

> Wonderful is the teacher, Sri Krishna;
> Wonderful are his deeds.
> Even the utterance of his holy name
> Sanctifies him who speaks and him who hears.

There comes a time in the growth of a spiritual aspirant when it becomes impossible for him to talk of anything but God, and if he hears of any worldly topics he runs away.

Sri Krishna says in the Gita:

> Mind and sense absorbed,
> I alone am the theme of their discourse:
> Thus delighting each other,
> They live in bliss and contentment.

18. *The sage Shandilya defines bhakti as avoiding all distracting thoughts, and taking delight only in the Atman.*

When devotion arises in the heart of a man, he naturally becomes free from all distracting thoughts, for he finds a greater delight in the thought of the Atman —the indwelling God—hidden in the shrine of his own heart. In other words, to find delight, satisfaction, and peace in the Atman is true devotion, according to Shandilya.

Sri Ramakrishna told how during his practice of spiritual disciplines he would meditate upon God as an ocean of Existence, pure Consciousness, and Bliss, covering the whole universe, and that he thought of himself as a fish swimming and diving in that ocean. Then he remarked that when this meditation deepens one actually experiences this ocean of *Sat-chit-ananda*—the ocean of Existence, pure Consciousness, and Bliss. Again Sri Ramakrishna would feel that he was a vessel dipped in that ocean—the indivisible ocean of Sat-chit-ananda—within him and outside him.

Sri Ramakrishna from his own experience would say, "Sometimes I feel 'Thou art I, and I am Thou'; and then, 'Thou art Thou'—there is no more 'ego' left."

Holy Mother once said that when she was initiated by Sri Ramakrishna she felt like a jar filled to the brim. Her heart was brimming with the bliss of God.

19. *Narada gives these as the signs of bhakti: When all thoughts, all words, and all deeds are given up to the Lord, and when the least forgetfulness of God makes one intensely miserable, then love has begun.*

After quoting the definitions of bhakti given by different sages, Narada sums up by harmonizing all those definitions of bhakti in this one. In short, Narada emphasizes complete self-surrender as bhakti. This ideal of self-surrender includes every kind of spiritual discipline.

In the first place, self-surrender means constant recollectedness of God. As Swami Vivekananda said, "Seek not God, but *see* him." God is omnipresent. The moment you think of God, convince yourself that you are actually in his presence. Then long for him and pray to him that he may reveal himself to you. Swami

Shivananda, a disciple of Sri Ramakrishna, used to tell us often, "Pray earnestly, day and night, with anguish in your heart, that you may have devotion to Him."

The Psalmist says, "Evening, and morning, and at noon, will I pray, and cry aloud: and he shall hear my voice." (Ps. 55:17)

In the Gospel according to St. Luke we read, "And he spake a parable unto them to this end, that men ought always to pray . . ." St. Paul said, "Pray without ceasing."

As you learn to surrender yourself to God, you "pray without ceasing," that is to say, all your deeds and thoughts are given up to the Lord.

In the words of Sri Krishna, in the Bhagavad-Gita:

> Give me your whole heart,
> Love and adore me,
> Worship me always,
> Bow to me only,
> And you shall find me:
> This is my promise
> Who love you dearly.
>
> Lay down all duties
> In me, your refuge.
> Fear no longer,
> For I will save you
> From sin and from bondage.

Self-surrender also means that *the least forgetfulness of God makes one miserable.*

There is a prayer of Sri Chaitanya:

Ah, how I long for the day
When an instant's separation from Thee,
  O Govinda,
Will be as a thousand years,
When my heart burns away with its desire
And the world, without Thee, is a heartless void.

20. *Examples exist of such perfect expressions of love.*

Narada, as he describes the nature of true love, declares in no uncertain terms that love for God in which one completely surrenders oneself to him is not a mere theoretical ideal; such exemplary men and women of God do exist. Narada in the next verse cites the example of the gopis, the shepherdesses of Brindavan, and their love for Krishna. One may say that this example is prehistoric. But many historical exemplars can be found among the followers of all religions, and they also exist today. In my own life, within my limited circle, I have witnessed such examples in the lives of a number of the disciples of Sri Ramakrishna. They were immersed in the bliss of this divine love, and taught us to pray only to attain pure love for God.

Sri Ramakrishna used to say to his disciples:

"When true yearning for God comes, then follows the sight of him, then rises the sun of knowledge in the heart. Yearn for him, and love him intensely! . . . The mother loves her child, the chaste wife loves her husband, the miser loves his wealth; let your love for God be as intense as these three loves combined—then shall you see him." (Gospel of Sri Ramakrishna)

He told his disciples how he himself prayed for devotion during a period of intense spiritual discipline: "O Mother, here is sin and here is virtue; take them both and grant me pure love for thee. Here is knowledge and here is ignorance; I lay them at thy feet. Grant me pure love for thee. Here is purity and here is impurity; take them both and grant me pure love for thee. Here are good works and here are evil works; I lay them at thy feet. Grant me pure love for thee." (Gospel of Sri Ramakrishna)

Narada cites the example:

21. *As the gopis of Braja had it.*

This refers to the episode of Sri Krishna and his divine play with the gopis, the shepherdesses of Brindavan (or Braja).

Love is intrinsically divine, as already stated, and finds its fulfillment when it is turned toward God. This divine love, again, is expressed in many forms (as we shall find explained in one of the later aphorisms). In the Srimad Bhagavatam, we find that Sri Krishna, the God of Love, was loved by Yasoda as her baby; to the shepherd boys Krishna was their beloved friend and playmate, and to the shepherd girls Krishna was lover and companion.

When Sri Krishna played on his flute, the shepherdesses were drawn to him like moths to the light. They would become forgetful of everything, unconscious even of their own bodies. They ran to him, drawn by his love.

In the same scripture we read: "Blessed are the shepherdesses of Brindavan. They are constantly remembering the Lord, for their hearts are forever united with him, even while they are milking, churning, washing, or doing household tasks. They sing the praises of the Lord Hari with a devoted and loving heart."

Sri Ramakrishna often went into samadhi when he heard the gopis mentioned, or thought of their intense love for Krishna.

Sri Ramakrishna said about the gopis:

"As the tiger devours other animals, so does the tiger of intense love and zeal for the Lord eat up lust, anger and other passions. The devotion of the gopis is the devotion of love, constant, unmixed, and unflinching."

Krishna, who gives delight to all and who is blissful in his own being, divided himself into as many Krishnas as there were shepherd girls and danced and played with them. Each girl felt the divine presence and divine love of Sri Krishna. Each felt herself the most blessed. Each one's love for Krishna was so absorbing that she felt herself one with Krishna, nay, knew herself to be Krishna. And wherever their eyes fell they saw only Krishna.

Swami Vivekananda wrote:

"Gopilila (the divine play of the gopis) is the acme of the religion of love, in which individuality vanishes and there is communion. It is in this *lila* that Sri Krishna shows what he teaches, 'Give up everything for me.' Go and take shelter under Brindavan lila to understand bhakti.

"Ah, the most marvelous passage of his life, the most difficult to understand until one has become perfectly chaste and pure—that most marvelous expansion of love, allegorized and expressed in that beautiful play of Brindavan, which none can comprehend but he who has become mad with, and drunk deep of, the cup of love! Who can conceive the throes of the love of the gopis—the shepherd girls—the very ideal of love, love that wants nothing, love that even does not care for heaven, love that does not care for anything in this world or in the world to come?

"The historian who records this marvelous love of the gopis is one who was born pure, the eternally pure Suka, the son of Vyasa. So long as there is selfishness in the heart, so long is love of God impossible; it is nothing but shop-keeping.

"Oh, for one, one kiss of those lips. One who has been kissed by thee—his thirst for thee increases forever, all sorrows vanish, and he forgets love for everything else but for thee and thee alone. . . . Ay, forget first love of gold, and name and fame and for this little trumpery world of ours. Then, only then, will you understand the love of the gopis, too holy to be attempted without giving up everything, too sacred to be conceived until the soul has become perfectly pure. People with ideas of sex, and of money, and of fame, bubbling up every minute in their hearts, daring to criticize or interpret the love of the gopis!

" . . . here is the very ecstasy of enjoyment, the drunkenness of love, where disciples and teachers and teachings and books, and even the ideas of fear and God and heaven—all these have become one. Everything else has been thrown away. What remains is the mad transport of love. In complete obliviousness to all else, the lover sees nothing in the world except that Krishna, and Krishna alone, for the face of every being has become a Krishna, and his own face looks like Krishna, and his own soul has become tinged with that Krishna color. . . . That indeed was the great Krishna."

22. *Although worshiping Krishna as their lover, the gopis never forgot his God-nature.*

We read in the Srimad Bhagavatam: "Once Krishna, to test their devotion to him, said to the gopis, 'O ye pure ones, your duties must be first to your husbands and children. Go back to your homes and live in their service. You need not come to me. For if you only meditate on me, you will gain salvation.' But the shepherd girls replied, 'O thou cruel lover, we desire to serve only thee! Thou knowest the scriptural truths, and thou dost advise us to serve our husbands and children. So let it be! We shall abide by thy teaching. Since thou art all in all, and art all, by serving thee we shall serve them also.' "

The truth taught here is that just as by watering the root of the tree, the branches also are nourished, so by pleasing the Lord, who dwells in the hearts of all, all beings are pleased.

In the same scripture we read how the gopis address Krishna, saying, "Thou art not only the darling baby of Yasoda, but Thou art the innermost Self in all beings."

The gopis, as stated above, attained their oneness with Krishna, the supreme state of transcendental consciousness, by loving the Lord as their one and only Beloved.

23. *If they did not have that knowledge that Krishna was God, then their love would have been similar to the base passion of a mistress for her paramour.*

24. *In lust there is only the desire for one's own pleasure; one's happiness does not consist in making the beloved happy.*

The nature of love is divine, and it finds its fulfillment only when it is directed toward God. In the *Imitation of Christ*, Thomas à Kempis puts these words into the mouth of the Lord, "Thy regard for thy friend ought to be grounded in Me; and for My sake is he to be beloved, whosoever he be. . . . Without Me, friendship has no strength, no continuance; neither is that love true and pure, which is not knit in Me."

There is a vast difference between love for God and love for creatures, when it is not grounded in love for God. The love of a mistress for her paramour is but another name for lust for flesh. Its basis is to find pleasure for oneself. In the Sanskrit language, its other name is *moha*, or delusion.

In divine love there is complete forgetfulness of the body, complete effacement of selfishness, and complete absorption in the Beloved. The one aim is to please the Beloved. Utter selflessness is the nature of this divine love.

IV

THE HIGHEST GOAL OF HUMAN LIFE

25. *Bhakti is greater than karma, greater than jnana,
greater than yoga (raja-yoga).*

In this and the succeeding eight aphorisms, Narada
emphasizes that supreme devotion is greater than the
other three paths—the paths of union through action,
through knowledge, or through meditation. This may
cause some misunderstanding. It may appear that
Narada is one-sided and that he prefers the path of devotion to the other paths to union. But on close exami-
nation, we shall find that Narada here does not refer
to the *path* of devotion as such, but to the ultimate end,
which is union with Brahman, the effect of supreme devotion.

As mentioned before, bhakti has two meanings—*the
realized goal*, and *the path which leads to the goal*.
Later Narada will explain the path—the disciplines
which lead to the goal.

As we stated at the beginning of this book, there are
four yogas or paths to union with God. These are: the
path of devotion, the path of knowledge, the path of
work, and the path of meditation. These four yogas,
however, cannot be separated into airtight compartments. In the teachings of the Bhagavad-Gita and of
Sri Ramakrishna, emphasis is laid upon harmonizing
all the yogas in one's life and not becoming one-sided.
In other words, one cannot really follow any one of

67

these four paths to the exclusion of the rest; only the aspirant may lay greater stress upon one or the other.

For instance, meditation is to be practiced as a discipline no matter which path the aspirant may follow. Also the aspirant must discriminate, and he is to be active as well; furthermore, the aspirant must have interest in and longing or love for the Ideal. Thus in reality, there is a combination of all yogas in every aspirant's life.

In this connection, again let me point out how the follower of the path of love and the follower of the path of knowledge reach the same result in the end. Perfect knowledge and supreme love become one.

There is, however, a slight distinction between the followers of the path of knowledge and of the path of devotion. The followers of the path of knowledge meditate from the beginning on their unity with Brahman. The followers of the path of devotion begin as dualists.

But as we analyze, we find that though the followers of the path of knowledge meditate on their unity with Brahman, still, in the path itself, there is duality—the meditator and the object of meditation.

A devotee begins as a dualist and, as a general rule, he does not willingly seek union with God. His one desire and longing is to have the vision of God and taste the bliss of communion with him.

Once, while I was seated at the feet of Maharaj, my master, a devotee approached him and asked, "Maharaj, there is a song sung by devotees, 'I want to taste sugar, but not to become sugar.' Should that be the attitude of a devotee?" Maharaj replied, "'I want to taste sugar, but not become sugar,' is for the man who has not yet tasted sugar. When a devotee begins to taste the sweetness of God, he will long to achieve oneness with him."

When this supreme love for God arises, love, lover, and the Beloved become one. There is the unitive knowledge of the Godhead. Supreme love and perfect knowledge are one.

Knowledge or jnana requires the idea of a distinction between the knower (meditator), the object of knowledge (Brahman), and the process of knowledge. However, to have the knowledge of God does not mean that God is the object and the knower is the subject. Immanuel Kant pointed out that as long as there is the least demarcation between the knower and the object of knowledge, the *thing-in-itself* remains unknown. Shankara, many centuries earlier, had also pointed out that as long as there is the least separation between the subject and the object of knowledge, and the process of knowledge, God remains unknown. But he stated that ultimately the spiritual aspirant transcends this dilemma; he called it *triputi-bheda*, the untying of the three knots of knowledge, and reaching "unified consciousness."[1]

Brahman or God is Sat-chit-ananda—Existence or eternal Reality, pure Consciousness, and pure Love and Bliss. These, however, are not attributes of Brahman. That which is Sat is the same as Chit, and the same as Ananda. Sat is identical with Brahman. Chit is identical with Brahman. Ananda is identical with Brahman. In the path of knowledge, emphasis is laid upon Chit, pure Consciousness; and in the path of devotion, em-

---

1 To quote Shankara: "Thus the wise man reaches that highest state, in which consciousness of subject and object is dissolved away and the infinite unitary consciousness alone remains—and he knows the bliss of *nirvana* while still living on earth."

phasis is laid upon Ananda—Love or Bliss. When the aspirant reaches the end, there is no longer any distinction between the Chit and Ananda. Then supreme love and unitive knowledge of Godhead become one and the same.

In the Bhagavad-Gita we read that Sri Krishna gave divine sight to his friend and disciple Arjuna, enabling him to have the direct experience of God in his universal form. Then Sri Krishna told Arjuna:

"Neither by study of the Vedas, nor by austerities, nor by alms-giving, nor by rituals can I be seen as you have seen me. But by single-minded and intense devotion, that Form of mine may be completely known and seen, and entered into." This refers to supreme love, which is the same as divine wisdom.

Why is bhakti considered as the greatest by Narada?

26. *For bhakti is the ultimate end and goal of spiritual life. All other paths lead a man to its realization.*

It has already been pointed out that supreme love and illumined knowledge of God are identical. To realize that supreme love which gives the unitive knowledge of the Godhead is therefore considered as the purpose and fruit of all spiritual disciplines.

Sri Krishna says in the Bhagavad-Gita:

> To love is to know me,
> My innermost nature,
> The truth that I am:
> Through this knowledge he enters
> At once to my Being.
> All that he does

Is offered before me
In utter surrender:
My grace is upon him,
He finds the eternal,
The place unchanging.

27. *Bhakti is the greatest also because God dislikes egotism and loves humility.*

God dislikes egotism means that as long as we have egotism and vanity, God remains hidden or covered within us. The man of God, who has attained the supreme love, transcends ego-consciousness.

In one of the Upanishads we read that a man of realization becomes *nativadi*, that is, he becomes humble and does not assert himself.

There is a prayer of Sri Chaitanya, which my master often repeated to me:

Be humbler than a blade of grass,
Be patient and forbearing like the tree,
Take no honor to thyself,
Give honor to all,
Chant unceasingly the name of the Lord.

In the Psalms we read: "Him that hath an high look and a proud heart will not I suffer," and in Proverbs: "Every one that is proud in heart is an abomination to the Lord."

Peter says: "God resisteth the proud, and giveth grace to the humble." Sri Krishna, describing the demonic tendencies in man, says: "Conceited, haughty, foolishly proud . . . these malignant creatures are full

71

of egotism, vanity, wrath . . . I cast them back, again and again, into the wombs of degraded parents, subjecting them to the wheel of birth and death."

This does not, however, mean that these are lost forever, or that God withholds his grace from them. After suffering throughout many births, they will ultimately learn to discriminate and devote themselves to God. It is the "ego" that keeps them blinded. It is true that both experiences of happiness and misery in life are great teachers, but misery is a greater teacher, for when a man is in the depths of misery and finds no way out, then it is that he turns toward God, knowing that God alone is the refuge.

God is not partial to anyone, nor does he withhold his grace from any; but as Sri Ramakrishna says, on high ground rain water does not accumulate. Similarly the grace of God is not felt by a proud man, who has "a high look."

The moment we learn to be humble we begin to feel His grace.

When Sri Krishna describes how he subjects those of a demonic nature "to the wheel of birth and death" so that they may learn to devote themselves to him, he is not contradicting himself, for he says elsewhere in the Bhagavad-Gita:

> My face is equal
> To all creation,
> Loving no one
> Nor hating any.
> Nevertheless,
> My devotees dwell
> Within me always:

I also show forth
And am seen within them.

28. *Some are of the opinion that knowledge is the
means to attain bhakti.*

Here, of course, *knowledge* does not refer to "the illumined knowledge of God," which is identical with
"supreme devotion." Knowledge here means understanding of the reasons why we need to pray or devote
ourselves to God. There has to be some knowledge of
the goal we wish to attain, and of some idea or ideal of
God; and of how in God alone there is fulfillment of
life. Buddha mentions "right understanding" as the
first step in his eightfold noble path to reach nirvana.
In the *Cloud of Unknowing*, we read, "Prayer may not
goodly be gotten in beginners or proficients, without
thinking before."

The faculty of reason has an important place in
spiritual life, though vain arguments must be avoided
by the aspirant.

29. *Others are of the opinion that knowledge and devotion are interdependent.*

This also is very true—knowledge and devotion are
like two wings with which the spiritual aspirant can
fly to spiritual heights. If love is not combined with intellect and will, it may turn into blind emotionalism;
and if intellect is not assisted by love and interest in
God, it becomes dry intellectualism. As we read in the
Cloud of Unknowing, "By the least longing a man is
led to be the servant of God, not by faultless deductions

73

of dialectics, but by the mysterious logic of the heart."

Both intellect and devotion must go hand in hand. First we must be convinced through the process of reasoning that God, the eternal Being, the pure Consciousness, the abiding Love and Bliss—is the innermost Self of our being, and then we must have interest in him and love for him in order to unfold the pure knowledge and supreme love, and thereby attain our union with him.

30. *Narada says that spiritual realization is its own fruit.*

Supreme love is identical with spiritual realization, which is its own fruit. Narada thereby indicates that the unfoldment of divinity, which is within, is not the effect of any other cause. That which is the effect of any other cause is bound to be something finite, because causation works within relativity and finitude. Spiritual realization is something eternal and infinite.

One may ask: What need is there of the spiritual disciplines? What need of the Vedas or the Bible or other spiritual teachings? They also are within relativity and bound by the law of causation. In short, they are all within what the Vedantists call *maya.*

But we must remember that there are two aspects of maya—*vidya* and *avidya.* Vidya is that which ultimately leads us beyond maya, and avidya is that which binds us more firmly to maya and greater ignorance. Scriptures, teachings, and spiritual disciplines belong to vidyamaya, which leads us to freedom from maya. It is not that illumined knowledge of God or supreme love is the effect of these disciplines and teachings. God is

74

already dwelling within and that pure knowledge which is one with supreme love is already there, being identical with God. But God, who is dwelling within, is covered by ignorance. Though spiritual disciplines as taught by the teachers and scriptures are finite, they remove ignorance, which is also finite. As the ignorance is removed, the divinity within us becomes unfolded.

Sri Ramakrishna used to give the illustration of a thorn stuck in one's flesh. One uses another thorn to take it out and then throws both away.

The Vedas say we must reach the stage when Vedas become no Vedas. Shankara says: "The Vedas, the Puranas, all scriptures and all living creatures only exist because the Atman exists. How then can any of them reveal the Atman, which is the revealer of everything?"

31 & 32. *A man cannot please a king by merely knowing about him and seeing his palace, nor can a man satisfy his hunger by the mere knowledge and sight of food; similarly a man cannot be satisfied by the knowledge or perception of God until love comes.*

The Bible tells us how some of Christ's disciples did not recognize his true nature, even though they were constantly together, until he revealed himself to them.

Jesus said to Thomas, "If ye had known me, ye should have known my Father also; and from henceforth ye know him and have seen him."

"Philip saith unto him, Lord, shew us the Father, and it sufficeth us. Jesus saith unto him, Have I been so long time with you, and yet hast thou not known

75

me, Philip? he that hath seen me hath seen the Father; and how sayest thou then, Shew us the Father? Believest thou not that I am in the Father, and the Father in me? the words that I speak unto you I speak not of myself: but the Father that dwelleth in me, he doeth the works. Believe me that I am in the Father and the Father in me: or else believe me for the very works' sake." (John 14:7-11)

Also let us remember that Jesus asked Peter, "Lovest thou me?"

Thus it is that when love comes God reveals himself.

One of the greatest indications of the truth that God incarnates as a human being is that he transfigures himself before his disciples, as, for instance, Jesus did. We read in the Gospel according to St. Matthew: "And after six days Jesus taketh Peter, James, and John his brother, and bringeth them up into an high mountain apart, and was transfigured before them: and his face did shine as the sun, and his raiment was white as the light."

In the eleventh book of the Bhagavad-Gita we find Sri Krishna revealing himself as God in his universal form to his beloved disciple and friend Arjuna. And he reveals himself to all those who love him dearly.

Sri Ramakrishna also underwent transfiguration before his beloved disciples many times. Years after his passing away, Swami Saradananda asked my master to look at the model of a statue of Sri Ramakrishna and see if he approved of it. Maharaj was then in a high spiritual mood, and he asked, "But which form of the Master?" because he had seen Sri Ramakrishna transfigured into many forms. Once, as a young boy, he saw him as Mother Kali and went into samadhi.

The Lord may come to us in many forms, but we do not always recognize him, unless he reveals himself to us and until we have deep love for him.

I shall relate a personal experience in this connection. Many years ago, four of us, *brahmacharis*, went on a pilgrimage to Badri-Narayana, in the Himalayas. One among us was Gurudas Maharaj, who was a westerner. At that time, the priests did not allow any westerner to go inside the shrine of a Hindu temple. When we arrived, we found many pilgrims seated in the courtyard of the temple; the doors were then closed. We also were seated in a corner of the courtyard with the other pilgrims. A few minutes later I saw a priest beckoning to me. As I approached him, he said, "Ask your friends also to come with me." He took us around by the side of the temple, opened the door and let us enter the innermost shrine. When other pilgrims wanted to enter, he said, "No, it is not time for you yet." And he shut the door. Then we saw this priest standing beside the deity. It did not occur to us then that as a general rule, no priest does this. He always stands facing the deity. After a few minutes of *darshan*, we were asked by the priest to go out, and then the door was locked again.

A little later, the head priest refused to allow us to enter the sanctum sanctorum, though he made arrangements for us to look at the deity from the door at a time when other pilgrims were not allowed to enter, so that our view would be unobstructed. And the head priest also gave us accommodation and sent us delicious sacramental food. We were there for three days and three nights as honored guests. During our stay we became acquainted with the few other priests who lived there.

But it seemed strange to us that we never saw the priest who took us to the innermost shrine. On our way back, we visited Swami Turiyananda, a disciple of Sri Ramakrishna, who was then living at Almora in the Himalayas, and we reported the incident to him. He said excitedly, "Ah! How foolish you are not to have recognized the Lord! It was He who appeared in that form and led you to the innermost shrine!"

33. *Therefore, those who desire to transcend all limitations and bondages (of birth, death, rebirth, of all the pairs of opposites in this relative world) must accept supreme love as the highest goal.*

"God alone can fill our soul." In him alone is immortal bliss. Until we reach this unitary consciousness, we remain subject to the bondages of birth and death, and to all the pairs of opposites—pleasure and pain, virtue and vice, and so forth.

When this supreme love arises, Brahman or God is experienced within the shrine of one's own heart, and the same Reality is seen in all.

Sri Ramakrishna said once to his disciples who were seated before him, "I see Rama, the supreme Being, seated before me in so many forms."

In the Chhandogya Upanishad we read, "The Infinite is below, above, behind, before, to the right, to the left. This Infinite is the Self. The Self [Atman] is below, above, behind, before, to the right, to the left. I am all this. One who knows, meditates upon, and realizes the truth of the Self—such a one delights in the Self, revels in the Self, rejoices in the Self."

Shankara, describing the state of an illumined soul

who has attained the unitary consciousness, says, "No matter what he is doing—walking, standing, sitting or lying down—the illumined seer whose delight is the Atman lives in joy and freedom."

This describes the illumined seer, who has attained the supreme love—the complete unfoldment of divinity. That must be the goal of all human beings.

V

HOW TO ATTAIN SUPREME LOVE

34. *The great teachers describe in hymns and songs the following as the means of attaining supreme love.*

I have translated the Sanskrit word *acharyas* as the great teachers. The word has a deep significance. Who is said to be a spiritual teacher? He who has directly experienced the truth of God, he who has attained that supreme love is the acharya, the real teacher. He is moved by compassion for his fellow beings and helps the spiritual aspirants to realize the same truth. There is power behind the words he speaks. Mere book learning is of no avail.

To quote Shankara: "Erudition, well-articulated speech, a wealth of words, and skill in expounding the scriptures—these things give pleasure to the learned, but they do not bring liberation.

"Study of the scriptures is fruitless as long as Brahman has not been experienced."

Now the question arises: What need is there to practice spiritual disciplines? For we have already shown (see aphorism 30) that supreme love or the experience of Brahman is not an effect nor is it dependent upon any cause. It is already an accomplished fact. The divinity is already there within each human soul, only there is ignorance covering it. As we read in the Gospel according to St. John: "And the Light shineth in darkness, and the darkness comprehended it not." Spiritual disciplines are needed to remove this darkness or ignorance.

This truth is also emphasized in another way by the doctrine of divine grace. As we read in the Katha Upanishad: "The Self is not known through study of the scriptures, nor through subtlety of the intellect, nor through much learning. Whom the Self chooses, by him is he attained. Verily unto him does the Self reveal His true being."

But whom does He choose? He chooses him who longs for Him. Sri Ramakrishna used to say, "Practice, practice the spiritual disciplines as taught by the guru, and then that longing and yearning for God will arise. The darkness of the night vanishes when the sun rises. Weep for Him, yearn with a longing heart, and the sun of knowledge will arise and darkness will vanish."

Shankara points out: "Faith, devotion, and constant union with God through prayer—these are declared by the sacred scriptures to be the seeker's direct means of liberation.

"A buried treasure is not uncovered by merely uttering the words 'Come forth.' You must follow the right directions, dig, remove the stones and earth from above it, and then make it your own. In the same way, the pure truth of the Atman, which is buried under maya and the effects of maya, can be reached by meditation, contemplation and other spiritual disciplines such as a knower of Brahman may prescribe—but never by subtle arguments."

From the quotation above, one might suppose that we reach that unfoldment through our own efforts, but as a matter of fact, through the practice of these disci-

81

plines we feel the grace of God. Every mystic who has had any kind of experience or realization, whether it is only an ecstasy, or the lower samadhi, or the highest transcendental consciousness, will admit that. Such experience flashes on the consciousness with a suddenness which makes him realize it is coming from beyond, as if a big magnet were drawing his mind into that experience beyond the normal consciousness. It is a direct experience of God and his grace.

Sri Ramakrishna used to tell his disciples, "The breeze of grace is blowing, set your sail to catch that breeze." And my master often said, "If you take one step toward God, he comes down a hundred steps toward you."

Also my master used to say, "A man may struggle for success in the world; he may succeed or he may fail. And even if he succeeds, it is only something fleeting. But in spiritual life, if a man struggles there is never any failure; and he achieves That which is eternal."

Narada has defined the goal, the true nature of supreme love. Now he is going to give us the methods by which that goal can be reached. There are many methods for attaining it. Narada summarizes all the various teachings of the acharyas, the illumined teachers, in the following aphorisms. One may adopt one, or several, or all of these methods to reach the goal.

They may be divided into two groups—negative and positive. Both are necessary, but in the way of divine love more emphasis is laid upon the positive aspect of the disciplines. Sri Ramakrishna used to say, "As you move toward the light, darkness is left behind." Or as we read in the Srimad Bhagavatam: "Be devoted to the

Lord, fix your heart firmly on the Lord, and that will bring forth instantaneously *vairagya*, or dispassion, and jnana, direct revelation of the Lord."

The following aphorism states the negative method:

35. *To attain supreme love, a man must renounce the objects of sense pleasure as well as attachment to them.*

What exactly is meant by the objects of sense pleasure and attachment to them?

Sri Ramakrishna used to refer to them as worldliness, and worldliness he would define as "lust and greed."

Renunciation of worldliness is essential if one would practice spiritual disciplines.

The secret is to wield the sword of discrimination. My master used to say, "Discriminate. Give up the fleeting pleasures in order to attain eternal bliss."

If we study the words of Christ, we shall find the same teaching of discrimination. We read in the Gospel according to St. Matthew: "Lay not up for yourselves treasures upon earth, where moth and rust doth corrupt, and where thieves break through and steal: But lay up for yourselves treasures in heaven, where neither moth nor rust doth corrupt, and where thieves do not break through nor steal: For where your treasure is there will your heart be also."

Once I asked Swami Turiyananda, "What is religion?" And he answered, "To make the heart and the lips the same." Therefore this renunciation of lust and greed must be not merely physical but mental as well.

HOW TO ATTAIN SUPREME LOVE

In the Bhagavad-Gita we read: "A man who renounces certain physical actions but still lets his mind
dwell on the objects of his sensual desire is deceiving
himself. He can only be called a hypocrite."

Some psychologists call this repression, which according to them creates complexes. So they advocate expression, that is, enjoyment of sense pleasures. But
that is not the remedy. The fact is that when a man
yields to the desires of the flesh he does not satisfy his
thirst for enjoyment—he increases it. Furthermore, the
senses have only limited capacities for enjoyment. The
mind continues to desire, but the senses are no longer
able to satisfy. Surely it must be admitted that this
leads to frustration and resultant complexes.

Sri Krishna was a great psychologist, and he tells us
not to be "hypocrites." What is the remedy he suggests? "The truly admirable man *controls* his senses by
the power of his will. All his actions are disinterested.
All are directed along the path to union with Brahman."

If a man does not make an effort to control himself
and lets himself yield to his passions, it becomes difficult to direct his thoughts to God. He may say a prayer
mechanically, but if his mind dwells on sense pleasures
it has no meaning. There is a parable of Sri Ramakrishna: "A man worked all day irrigating his field.
After laboring for many hours, he looked at the field
and found it still dry, for all the water had run off
through rat holes."

So Narada advocates not merely renunciation of the
objects of sense pleasures but of attachment to them as
well.

In the next aphorism we find the positive aspect.

36. (*Supreme love is attained*) *by uninterrupted and constant worship of God.*

37. *By hearing of and singing the glory of the Lord, even while engaged in the ordinary activities of life.*

This is the positive method, uninterrupted worship of God. In other words, to keep mind and heart in God constantly and unceasingly is a stage to be achieved by practice of the spiritual disciplines. You walk with God, you eat with him, you sleep with him. You then live always in the awareness of the presence of God. Brother Lawrence said: "In order to know God, we must often think of him; and when we come to love him we shall then also think of him often; for our heart will be with our treasure."

Sri Krishna says in the Bhagavad-Gita:

"When a yogi has meditated upon me unceasingly for many years, with an undisturbed mind, I am easy of access to him because he is always absorbed in me."

It takes many years of practice to become established in the thought of God with an undisturbed mind.

As the great yogi Patanjali says, "Practice becomes firmly grounded when it has been cultivated for a long time, uninterruptedly, with earnest devotion."

Shankara points out a great truth, that if a man struggles sincerely and earnestly for the supreme goal he is already as good as a siddha, a perfected soul.

Now the question is: How can we arrive at the state in which we shall be able to keep mind and heart in God uninterruptedly?

The methods are varied: Meditation upon God in

any chosen aspect by the aspirant, chanting the name of the Lord, ritualistic worship, singing praises of the Lord, study of the scriptures and meditation upon the meanings conveyed therein, service to God's devotees, service to God in mankind, doing one's allotted duties as acts of worship—all these, as well as any special practices given by one's own teacher, are the methods which will lead the aspirant to his goal.

Sri Ramakrishna gives many illustrations to show how an aspirant can keep his mind in God, even though he may be engaged in other duties: a village maiden carrying water on her head, well-balanced, with her mind concentrated on the water vessel, yet at the same time gossiping with other women; a chaste wife awaiting her husband's arrival with her mind concentrated on him, while at the same time cooking meals and nursing her baby.

All schools of thought lay great stress upon repeating the name of God and meditating upon its meaning, as an aid in keeping our minds constantly on God.

It is the general belief among all Vedantists, no matter to which school they may belong, that the name and the chosen ideal of God bearing that name are identical.

Patanjali says concerning God, "The word which expresses him is Om. The word must be repeated with meditation upon its meaning. Hence comes knowledge of the *Purusha* [Atman] and destruction of the obstacles to that knowledge."

To quote the Katha Upanishad in this connection:

"Of that goal which all the Vedas declare, which is implicit in all penances, and in pursuit of which men lead lives of continence and service, of that will I briefly speak. It is Om.

"This syllable is Brahman. This syllable is indeed supreme. It is the strongest support. It is the highest symbol. He who knows it is reverenced as a knower of Brahman."

And in the Mundaka Upanishad we read:

"Affix to the Upanishad, the bow incomparable, the sharp arrow of devotional worship; then, with mind absorbed and heart melted in love, draw the arrow and hit the mark—the imperishable Brahman.

"Om is the bow, the arrow is the individual being, and Brahman is the target. With a tranquil heart, take aim. Lose thyself in him, even as the arrow is lost in the target."

There are other symbols or names of God besides the word Om. As Sri Chaitanya says in his prayer:

Various are thy names, O Lord,
In each and every name thy power resides.
No times are set, no rites are needful, for chanting
   of thy name,
So vast is thy mercy.

God's name is called the mantra. As there are various names, there are various mantras, depending on the particular aspect of God a devotee chooses to worship. The teacher gives the disciple the mantra at the ceremony called *diksha,* or initiation. The essence of the disciple's Chosen Ideal is concentrated in the mantra, in the form of a sound symbol. These sound symbols express the deepest spiritual experiences of the sages and seers. To repeat the mantra, meditating on its meaning, implies that the aspirant must try to feel the presence of God within himself as he chants the name.

HOW TO ATTAIN SUPREME LOVE

During the ceremony of initiation, the teacher transmits spiritual power with the help of the mantra. As the name is repeated, the spiritual power with which it is charged becomes evident to the disciple.

To quote from the prayer of Sri Chaitanya again:

O Name, stream down in moonlight on the lotus
    heart,
Opening its cup to knowledge of thyself.
O self, drown deep in the waves of his bliss,
Chanting his name continually,
Tasting his nectar at every step
Bathing in his name, that bath for weary souls.

Both the Old and the New Testaments recommend the spiritual practice of chanting God's name:

"O magnify the Lord with me, and let us exalt his name together." (Psalms) "Let us offer the sacrifice of praise to God continually, that is, the fruit of our lips giving thanks to his name." (Hebrews)

"For whosoever shall call on the name of the Lord shall be saved." (Romans)

And in the Gospel according to St. John: "Verily, verily, I say unto you, Whatsoever ye shall ask the Father in my name, he will give it to you. Hitherto you have asked nothing in my name: ask, and ye shall receive, that your joy may be full."

The Jesus Prayer, a form of mantra, is recognized in the Eastern Orthodox Church. Its practice is explained in two remarkable books, *The Way of a Pilgrim* and its sequel *The Pilgrim Continues His Way*, which record the spiritual pilgrimage of a Russian devotee in the nineteenth century:

"The continuous interior Prayer of Jesus is a constant uninterrupted calling upon the divine Name of Jesus with the lips, in the spirit, in the heart; while forming a mental picture of his constant presence, and imploring his grace during every occupation, at all times, in all places, even during sleep. The appeal is couched in these terms, 'Lord Jesus Christ, have mercy on me.' One who accustoms himself to this appeal experiences as a result so deep a consolation and so great a need to offer the prayer always, that he can no longer live without it, and it will continue to voice itself within him of its own accord. . . .

"Many so-called enlightened people regard this frequent offering of one and the same prayer as useless and even trifling, calling it mechanical and a thoughtless occupation of simple people. But unfortunately they do not know the secret which is revealed as a result of this mechanical exercise, they do not know how this frequent service of the lips imperceptibly becomes a genuine appeal of the heart, sinks down into the inward life, becomes a delight, becomes, as it were, natural to the soul, bringing it light and nourishment and leading it on to union with God."

To sum up this teaching of uninterrupted and constant worship of God, in the words of Vivekananda:

"Day and night think of God, and as far as possible think of nothing else. The daily necessary thoughts can all be thought through God. Eat to Him, drink to Him, sleep to Him, see Him in all. Talk of God to others—this is most beneficial.

"When the whole soul pours in a continuous current to God, when there is no time to seek money or name or fame, no time to think of anything but God, then

89

will come into your heart that infinite, wonderful bliss of love. All desires are but beads of glass. True love of God increases every moment and is ever new—it is to be known by feeling it. Love is the easiest of disciplines. It waits for no logic; it is natural. We need no demonstration, no proof. Reasoning is limiting something by our own minds. We throw a net and catch something, and then say that we have demonstrated it. But never, never, can we catch God in a net."

Vivekananda himself set us an example in his love for his master, Sri Ramakrishna. Sri Ramakrishna loved Naren deeply. Once, perhaps to test young Naren, Sri Ramakrishna completely ignored him for months and would not speak to him. Then one day the Master asked Naren why he continued to come to see him when he knew that he was completely ignored. Naren replied, "I come to see you, because I love you." Love, true love must be motiveless.

38. *The principal means of attaining bhakti is the grace of a great soul.*

39. *It is hard to obtain the grace of a great soul, because it is hard to recognize such a one; but if a man receives his grace, the effect is infallible.*

40. *Through the grace of God alone an aspirant obtains the grace of a great soul.*

A great teacher, as already explained, is one who has attained union with Brahman. He is a man of God. We read in the Upanishads, "Verily a knower of Brahman has become one with Brahman." To obtain the grace of such a guru is the same as having the grace of God. Sri Ramakrishna used to say, "There is but one guru, and he is Sat-chit-ananda, that is God—who is the immortal Being, the pure Consciousness, and abiding Love and Bliss. Human gurus (who have attained the illumined knowledge of God) are like so many pipes through which the water of the same lake pours."

We read in the Srimad Bhagavatam: "Spiritual discrimination, virtuous deeds, sacrifices, study, austerity, repetition of the sacred mantras, resort to places of pilgrimage, righteous conduct—all these are aids to spiritual unfoldment: but the greatest help is the society of the holy, for by serving the saints and associating with them one cuts asunder the roots of ignorance and attachment. Many have attained the highest illumination, not by the study of the Vedas, nor yet by the practice of austerities, but merely by loving and serving the men of God."

The guru is he who opens the divine sight of the disciple. He is like a boat that takes us across the ocean of worldliness.

In the Vishwa-Sara Tantra, we find the following chant to the guru:

Him I bow down to, the perfect guru,
Who is absorbed in the bliss of Brahman,
Who can bestow that bliss upon others,
Who is free from our earthly bondage,
Who is the Self of the highest wisdom,
Who is beyond life's sweet and bitter,
Who is airlike, untouched by evil.
Often the scriptures speak of his nature,

91

HOW TO ATTAIN SUPREME LOVE

Saying "That art Thou," calling him changeless,
Pure, eternal, the One without second,
Witness of all the mind's moods and motions—
How shall thought compass or tongue describe him?

In this hymn we find the characteristics of a great
soul.

Even the divine incarnations, the sons of God, and
the prophets had to have gurus. In spite of the fact that
the divine incarnations are born with the knowledge of
their oneness with God, they become the disciples of
gurus. Krishna, Christ, Buddha, and Ramakrishna had
gurus.

The divine incarnations show us the way to ascend
toward Godhead; and the first thing needed is the grace
of a great soul.

Ralph Waldo Emerson, in his essay "Uses of Great
Men," speaks thus:

"It costs a beautiful person no exertion to paint her
image on our eyes. It costs no more for the wise soul
to convey his quality to other men. . . . With the great
our thoughts and manners become equally great. There
needs but one wise man in a company and all are wise
—so rapid is the contagion. . . . Great men are a colly-
rium to clear one's eyes of egotism. This is the key to
the power of great men—their spirit diffuses itself."

I have already quoted Vivekananda on the need for
a guru, but it is worth repeating, "Take refuge in some
soul who has already broken his bondage, and in time
he will free you through his grace."

Through the grace of the guru, which is the same as
the grace of God, an aspirant attains supreme love, and
union with Brahman.

It is said that "if a man receives his grace, the effect is infallible." In the Mahanirvana Tantra, we read, "The moment a disciple receives initiation with the mantra, the sacred name of God, from the guru, he becomes united with Brahman."

We know either historically or traditionally how divine incarnations, like Krishna, Christ, and Buddha transformed sinners into saints by touch. In the case of Sri Ramakrishna we know how he transformed drunkards and prostitutes into saints. I have had the blessed fortune to meet one such soul, Girish Ghosh. In his presence one could feel holiness.

Also we have witnessed how Holy Mother, Swamis Vivekananda, Brahmananda, Premananda, and others transformed the lives of sinners, and they became holy men and women.

That the effect of this grace from a guru is infallible was confirmed by my master when talking to one of his disciples. Maharaj said to this disciple, "What is to happen to you after death, I have already provided for. [Meaning that at least at the moment of death, the disciple would realize God and go to him, set free from the bondages of birth, death, and rebirth.] But if you want to realize that bliss of liberation while living, you must struggle and practice."

It is like getting into a train. You are sure to reach your destination, asleep or awake. But keep awake and enjoy the scenery on the way.

This same disciple at one time asked the permission of Maharaj to live in solitude and practice austerities. But Maharaj knew his weaknesses, and so he said, "Why do you have to practice austerities? We have done all that for you." And Maharaj asked this disciple

93

to love him. On three occasions he asked him simply to love him.

To love the guru is to love God. The mind thinking of the guru automatically begins to think of the chosen ideal of God.

As already stated, the guru gives divine sight to his disciples. In the presence of our master, Maharaj, we all felt how simple and easy it was to realize God. The guru makes the disciples realize the truth that God is his very own, that he is nearer than the nearest, ever present within as the Inner Ruler (*Antaryamin*).

Now a pertinent question arises. Among the disciples of great souls, there are some who seem to go astray and become subject to lust and greed. Such instances are even to be found among the disciples of divine incarnations. Also it is found that some who have even had God-vision seem to become worldly-minded afterward. How is this possible?

The answer to this is what the Hindus call *prarabdha karma*, the effects of the deeds of a past life, the tendencies which need to be worked out. Such people do not completely forget their past association or their past knowledge. They are reborn, and with redoubled energy they gain self-control and devote themselves to God.

Sri Ramakrishna said to one of his disciples, who at one time became troubled in his conscience: "You have the grace of your guru. Why should you fear? Take courage. He who has the grace of a guru cannot be drowned in the ocean of worldliness, even though storms of craving may arise. The guru will lift him up."

According to the theologians of Christendom, Judas,

the disciple who betrayed Jesus, is supposed to have lost the grace of Christ. But the Hindus do not believe it to be so. The Hindus believe that Judas also was lifted up to the Father in heaven, because he had the grace of his guru, Christ—an incarnation of God.

However, all these instances of disciples who go astray are examples to teach us to be on our guard and to be alert throughout our lives.

Let us remember the Lord's Prayer, "Lead us not into temptation"; and Sri Ramakrishna's prayer: "O Mother Divine, may we not be bewildered by your world-bewitching maya."

It is said in the Chandi, a sacred scripture of the Hindus, that even the gods prayed to Divine Mother, "The whole world, O Mother, is bewitched by you. It is only by pleasing you that anyone can escape from the misery of the bondages of birth and death, and of the pairs of opposites, realizing the truth of God."

What are the temptations into which God may lead us? What is the world-bewitching maya of Divine Mother? It is God's creation through his power, the Divine Mother. The outgoing senses seek to enjoy the pleasures of this created world, forgetting that God, the source of freedom and bliss, is within each of us.

Now let us consider the first part of aphorism 39. *It is hard to obtain the grace of a great soul, because it is hard to recognize such a one.*

Jesus points out clearly why it is hard to recognize a great soul:

" . . . John came neither eating nor drinking, and they say, He hath a devil. The Son of Man came eating and drinking, and they say, Behold a man gluttonous, and a winebibber, a friend of publicans and sinners."

My master used to say, "How many are ready? Yes, many people come to us. We have the treasure to offer them, but they only want potatoes, onions, and egg-plants."

In other words, one has to be thirsty to appreciate a cool drink. "Seek and ye shall find."

In the Katha Upanishad we read: "To many it is not given to hear of the Self. Many, though they hear of it, do not understand it. Wonderful is he who speaks of it. Intelligent is he who learns of it. Blessed is he who, taught by a good teacher, is able to understand it.

"The truth of the Self cannot be fully understood when taught by an ignorant man. . . . Subtler than the subtlest is this Self, and beyond logic. Taught by a teacher who knows the Self and Brahman as one, a man leaves vain theory behind and attains to truth."

We read in the Gospel according to St. Matthew:

"And he [Jesus] told them many things in parables, saying: 'A sower went out to sow. And as he sowed, some seeds fell along the path, and the birds came and devoured them. Other seeds fell on rocky ground, where they had not much soil, and immediately they sprung up, since they had no depth of soil, but when the sun rose they were scorched; and since they had no root they withered away. Other seeds fell upon thorns, and the thorns grew up and choked them. Other seeds fell on good soil and brought forth grain, some a hundred fold, some sixty, some thirty. He who has ears, let him hear."

So again we find Jesus saying, "Neither cast ye your pearls before swine." (Luke 7:6)

As Shankara very truly points out:

"Only through God's grace may we obtain those three rarest advantages—human birth, the longing for liberation, and discipleship to an illumined teacher."

When there comes the longing for liberation, when an aspirant becomes thirsty for God-vision, the field is ready for sowing the seed, and he receives the grace of the guru. When a man sincerely and earnestly seeks spiritual life, the transmitter of spiritual power must come.

41. *There is no difference between God and his devotees.*

God dwells in all beings in his infinitude; that is to say, one, infinite, absolute Reality—Brahman—dwells equally in all beings and everywhere. There is a saying in Sanskrit, "He dwells equally in Brahma, the creator, and in an inanimate object, such as a pillar." But there is a difference in the degree of his manifestations. In human beings he has a greater manifestation. Therefore it is said, "Blessed is this human birth." Because a human being has the opportunity and the power to realize God and reach union with him. But of all human beings God's most perfect manifestation is in his devotees, who have known him, who have talked with him, and who have become one with him. After having become one with him, the devotees remain as lovers of God, their enchantingly beloved Lord. God is not partial to anybody. He loves us all, but he considers his devotees as his very own. The devotees alone know and experience the overwhelming love of God.

In the Srimad Bhagavatam, the Lord speaks to the

sage Durbasa, "I love my devotees and I am a willing slave in my love. How can it be otherwise, since these devotees of mine willingly sacrifice everything for my sake? They have surrendered themselves completely unto me."

Sri Ramakrishna used to say, "Bhagavat, Bhakta, Bhagavan—the scriptures, the devotees, and the Lord are one and the same." Once he had a vision: A ray of light emanating from the image of Lord Krishna touched him and a scripture—showing him that these three are one and the same.

In the Mundaka Upanishad we read:

"The sage knows Brahman, the support of all, the pure effulgent being in whom is contained the universe. They who worship the sage, and do so without thought of self, cross the boundary of birth and death."

The devotees are a class by themselves, belonging to no particular caste, or race, or nationality, or sect of any particular religion. They are neither Hindus, nor Christians, nor Moslems, nor Jews—they are just men and women of God—rising above all barriers of caste or religion. Therefore, to receive grace from any of God's devotees is the same as having the grace of God.

42. *Seek therefore the mercy of a great soul.*

As already indicated, if a man has longing for God and yearns for his love, he finds a guru who can lead him in the spiritual path and show him the way to divine love.

So what is most important for an aspirant is to create a longing for God through discrimination. As

APHORISM 42

Shankara points out, "Even though this longing for liberation may be present in a slight or moderate degree, it will grow intense through the grace of the teacher, and through the practice of renunciation and of virtues such as tranquillity, etc. And it will bear fruit."

VI

SEEK HOLY COMPANY

43. *Shun evil company, by all means.*

Avoid evil company, especially at the beginning of spiritual life. Sri Ramakrishna says, "The young plant needs to be hedged around to protect it from being eaten up by stray animals. When the plant grows into a huge tree, then it gives shelter to all."

Evil company does not only mean association with worldly-minded people; it also refers to avoiding all objects of temptation. There is a prayer in the Upanishads:

With our ears may we hear what is good,
With our eyes may we behold thy righteousness.
Tranquil in body, may we who worship thee find
    rest.

There is a saying, "Open the eye of Spirit and see that Brahman is all."

We find that great souls make no distinction between the sinner and the saint. If men surrender themselves to the mercy of a great soul, they will be lifted up and become saints in their turn, even though they may have committed grave sins.

Sri Ramakrishna used to say, "God dwells in all, but you do not hug a tiger." However, in the presence of a man of God, even the tiger loses his ferocity and becomes like a lamb.

I personally experienced a strange phenomenon in the life of Maharaj, my master. One day in Madras as he was walking with another young disciple and myself a mad bull suddenly appeared a few yards away from us, approached with lowered head, and was about to charge. There was no time to run. My brother and I, in order to protect Maharaj, tried to step in front of him. But he raised his arms, pushed us behind him, and stood still, facing the bull. Then the bull calmed down, shook its head from side to side, and let us pass.

44. *Evil company should be shunned, because it leads to lust, anger, delusion, forgetfulness of the goal, and ultimate ruin.*

45. *These passions may at first remain like ripples, but evil company makes them rise to huge ocean waves.*

We are all born with *samskaras*, or impressions of our past deeds and thoughts; and we also create new impressions by our deeds and thoughts in the present life. Some are good and others are bad. We are all a mixture of good and evil. These samskaras of our past as well as of our present life are like seeds. If you keep holy company, it will give the good seeds an opportunity to grow, and the evil seeds will remain dormant. Hence the importance of associating with the holy and avoiding evil company.

There is a verse in the Bhagavad-Gita:

101

Thinking about sense-objects
Will attach you to sense-objects;
Grow attached and you become addicted;
Thwart your addiction, it turns to anger;
Be angry, and you confuse your mind;
Confuse your mind, you forget the lesson of
    experience;
Forget experience, you lose discrimination;
Lose discrimination, and you miss life's
    only purpose.

It is worth quoting Shankara also in this connection. "Know that the deluded man who walks the dreadful path of sense-craving, moves nearer to his ruin with every step. And know this to be true also—that he who walks the path indicated by his teacher, who is his truest well-wisher, and by his own better judgment, reaps the highest fruit of the knowledge of Brahman.

"If you really desire liberation, hold the objects of sense-enjoyment at a distance, like poison; and keep drinking in with delight such virtues as contentment, compassion, forgiveness, straightforwardness, tranquillity and self-control, as if they were nectar."

46. *Who indeed overcomes maya? He who gives up all attachment, who serves the great ones, and who is freed from the sense of "I and mine."*

What is maya? Maya, here, refers to ignorance that hides the Reality. Man's true nature is divine, but through some inscrutable power, known as maya, or ignorance, that divinity within us remains covered. The Self, the Atman, is one with Brahman. That is

102

the one unchangeable Reality within us. But through ignorance, the Self becomes identified with the non-Self—body, mind, senses, and sense-organs—and is not aware of his own divinity, considering himself finite, limited, and bound. This maya, or ignorance, is a matter of fact. The coupling of the real and the unreal, produced by our ignorance, is a process universally evident in our daily lives. Shankara points out that it is obvious and needs no proof that the object which is the non-Self and the subject which is the Self are opposed to each other, like light and darkness, and cannot be identified—still less their respective attributes. Yet, through some inscrutable power, a man, who in reality is the unchangeable, blissful Atman, superimposes upon himself the nature and attributes of the non-Self, coupling the real and the unreal; and as a matter of course he identifies himself with the body's mental and physical attributes and actions. We say, "I am fat," or "I am tired," without ever stopping to consider what this "I" is.

We go further. We claim purely external objects and conditions for our own. We announce that "I am a Democrat," or that "This house is mine." We identify our ego, more or less, with every object in the universe. And all the while the inner Self, the indwelling God, looks on, utterly detached from these moods and antics—yet making them all possible by lending to the mind the light of consciousness without which maya could not exist. This maya again is universal. It is in the intelligent, learned man, as well as in the ignorant. Only when knowledge dawns, this being the direct experience of the Atman, only then does this maya vanish.

103

SEEK HOLY COMPANY

In the Bhagavad-Gita, Sri Krishna says:

> How hard to break through
> Is this, my maya,
> Made of the gunas!
> But he who takes refuge
> Within me only
> Shall pass beyond maya:
> He, and no other.

To take refuge in God, to surrender ourselves completely to him, is the way to go beyond maya. We have already considered this ideal of self-surrender.

Now let us consider what else Narada has to say about the way in which this maya can be overcome.

He who gives up all attachment. What is this attachment? It is attachment to worldliness, which has been defined in two words by Sri Ramakrishna: "lust and greed." My master used to explain the practice of austerity as controlling the passions and restraining the sense-organs from going toward their object. This needs struggle and practice on the part of the spiritual aspirant.

To quote the Bhagavad-Gita in this connection. Arjuna asks:

"Krishna, you describe this yoga as a life of union with Brahman. But I do not see how this can be permanent. The mind is so very restless."

Arjuna continues:

> Restless man's mind is,
> So strongly shaken
> In the grip of the senses:

Gross and grown hard
With stubborn desire
For what is worldly.
How shall he tame it?
Truly, I think
The wind is no wilder.

Sri Krishna answers: "Yes, Arjuna, the mind is restless, no doubt, and hard to subdue. But it can be brought under control by constant practice, and by the exercise of dispassion. Certainly, if a man has no control over his ego, he will find this yoga difficult to master. But a self-controlled man can master it, if he struggles hard, and uses the right means."

St. Augustine referred to this as "steadfast self-discipline, and cleansing of the soul."

In the Chhandogya Upanishad we read: "When the food is purified, the heart becomes pure. When the heart is pure, there is constant recollectedness of God."

What is meant by "food" being purified? Food refers not only to what we eat but also to what we gather through the doors of the senses. It is easy to eat pure food. Physical purity is easily achieved. But the most important thing is to attain mental purity, purity of the heart. The great ones who have attained it tell us that we do not have to run away from sense-objects or withdraw from the world, but that we must move among sense-objects without attachment or aversion. Thus it is that food becomes purified.

And when food becomes purified, the heart becomes purified, and then comes constant recollectedness of God.

Constant recollectedness, in this connection, means

the state in which the mind runs toward God, like a steady stream, without any break caused by any sort of distraction; the illustration given is of "oil poured from one vessel to another."

When the mind thus runs in a steady stream toward God, then the aspirant attains supreme love and thereby reaches his union with God.

Christ, in the Sermon on the Mount, said, "Blessed are the pure in heart, for they shall see God."

The sign of this purity is constant recollectedness of God, and that is the supreme love for God.

"The mind must always think of the Lord." It is of course very hard in the beginning to think of the Lord always, but with every new effort the power to do so grows stronger in us.

The bhakta, or devotee, achieves dispassion in a smooth and natural way. Let me give an example from the ordinary life of worldly-minded people. A man loves a woman; after a while he is attracted by another woman and begins to love her, and he lets the first woman go. She is wiped out of his mind smoothly, gently, without his feeling the want of her at all.

St. Francis de Sales in his *Treatise on the Love of God*, says, "Amongst all loves, God's is so to be preferred that we must always stand prepared in mind to forsake them all, for that alone."

My master often urged us to practice, practice. It is through the practice of the presence of God in the heart that we begin to feel the overwhelming love of God for us, and love for him comes naturally. "Practice, practice, meditate, meditate"—these are the words of my master, still ringing clearly in my ears.

In the words of Vivekananda: "So this love for the pleasures of the senses and of the intellect is all made dim and thrown aside and cast into the shade by the love of God Himself. . . . Bhakti Yoga is the science of higher love. It shows us how to direct it; it shows us how to control it, how to manage it, how to use it, how to give it a new aim, as it were, and from it obtain the highest and most glorious results, that is, how to make it lead us to spiritual blessedness. Bhakti Yoga does not say, 'Give up'; it only says, 'Love—love the Highest.' And everything low naturally falls away from him, the object of whose love is the Highest."

We then live in the world like the lotus leaf—water drops away from it though it grows in water. Live in the world, but be not of it.

He . . . who serves the great ones. We have already explained the need for a guru, a spiritual guide. The principal means of attaining supreme love is through the grace of a guru.

The service of the guru is very important for the attainment of supreme love and wisdom. In one of the Hindu scriptures we read, "He who serves the guru attains the knowledge of Brahman which is in his possession, just as only he who digs with a spade gets water." The guru has the power to give liberation to his disciple.

The scriptures reveal wonderful truths; but without exemplars of these truths, the truths do not become living. Service to such exemplars is necessary for spiritual aspirants.

According to the Bhagavad-Gita, the seeker must do three things: He must prostrate before the guru— which means he must approach him humbly with a

107

heart full of longing to realize God. Then he must question him. When the guru instructs him, he should not just accept his words at face value but try to understand the teachings in order to remove all doubts from his mind. Also, he must give personal service.

To give personal service to the guru, though very important, does not necessarily mean service in a physical sense. In one of the Upanishads we read, "Hear of the truth of Brahman from the lips of a guru, then reason upon it, and lastly meditate upon the truth as instructed by him."

Thus service to the guru also means following his teachings. Swami Shivananda, one of the disciples of Sri Ramakrishna, once said, "Do you think that those of you who attend on me personally are the only ones who are serving me? Those who are in different centers [of the Ramakrishna Order] and even in far-off countries, though they do not see me, are also serving the Lord and serving me by serving the cause of our Master, and by the practice of contemplation and meditation."

He who . . . is freed from the sense of "I and mine." It has already been explained that maya is ignorance. Our true nature is divine, pure, free, and enlightened. But it is maya, the darkness of ignorance, which covers this light of Brahman within.

There is a similar truth taught in Zen. I quote here "The Song of Zazen" by Hakuin.

> All beings are primarily Buddhas,
> Like water and ice,
> There is no ice apart from water;
> There are no Buddhas apart from beings.

108

APHORISM 46

Not knowing how close the Truth is to them,
Beings seek for it afar—What a pity!

It is like those who being in water
Cry out for water, feeling thirst.
It is like the rich man's son,
Who has lost his way among the poor.

The reason why beings transmigrate through the
  six worlds
Is because they are lost in the darkness of
  ignorance—
Wandering from darkness to darkness,
How can they ever be free from birth and death?[1]

And the first begotten son of this darkness of ignorance is the sense of ego, the sense of "I and mine."
Sri Ramakrishna used to say, "When the ego dies,
all troubles cease." The clouds cover the light of the
sun. The moment the clouds move away, the sun
becomes visible. The ego is like that cloud covering
the light of the Atman or Brahman. When, through
the grace of the guru, and by following his instructions, the ego disappears, the truth of God becomes
revealed.

St. Francis de Sales writes in his *Letters to Persons
in Religion*, "God wants you wholly and without re-
serve, and to the very utmost stripped and denuded
of self."

The difference between Brahman and the individual
soul is created by the sense of "I" which stands be-

1 On Zazen Wasan Hakuin's "Song of Zazen" Lenkei Shibayama, translated by Sumika Kudo Kyoto.

tween. If you hold a stick on the surface of a lake, the water will appear to be divided into two parts, but in reality the water is one. It appears as two because of the stick. The sense of "I" is that stick, which separates us from God.

What is this sense of "I"? That which says, "I am this, I am that. I am intelligent, I possess so much wealth, I am great and powerful." How to get rid of this "I," and the sense of "I and mine"?

Sri Ramakrishna gives some very practical instructions on this point:

First, he explains that it is only in samadhi that the ego disappears completely. Then he says: "It generally clings to us. We may discriminate a thousand times, but the sense of 'I' is bound to return again and again. You may cut the branches of a fig tree today, but tomorrow you will see that new twigs are sprouting. If this sense of 'I' will not leave, then let it stay as the servant of God. 'O God! Thou art my Lord, I am thy servant!' Think in this way: 'I am his servant, I am his devotee.' There is no harm in this kind of 'I.' . . . Through prayer and repetition of his holy name with extreme longing, God can be reached without fail. . . . If this attitude of a servant be genuine and perfect, then passion and anger will drop off leaving only a scar in the mind. This 'I' of a devotee does no harm to any creature. It is like a sword which, after touching the philosopher's stone, is turned to gold. The sword retains the same form but it cannot cut or injure anyone. The dry leaves of the coconut tree drop off in the wind, leaving a mark on the trunk; that mark proves that there was a leaf there at one time. Similarly, the scar of the sense of 'I' remains in the mind of one who has realized God, but his whole nature is transformed into that of an innocent child. The child's sense of 'I' is not attached to worldly objects."

Furthermore, Sri Ramakrishna continues, "A householder should take care of his children, but at the same time he should think of them as Baby Krishnas, or as children of God. Serve your father as God, and your mother as Divine Mother. . . . Serve God who dwells in all beings."[1]

Sri Ramakrishna also taught this prayer:

I am the machine, Thou art the operator.
I am the house, Thou art the householder.
I speak as Thou makest me speak.
I act as Thou makest me act.

The aspirant must try to free himself from the idea that he is the doer.

47. (Who indeed overcomes maya?) *He who lives in solitude, cuts through the bondages of this world, goes beyond the three gunas, and depends upon the Lord even for his living.*

There are a few beautiful passages in the Kaivalya Upanishad which can be quoted here as a commentary on the above aphorism.

"Retire into solitude. Seat yourself on a clean spot and in an erect posture, with the head and neck in a straight line. Be indifferent to the world. Control all

1 *The Gospel of Sri Ramakrishna,* revised by Swami Abhedananda, from M's original English text (New York: Vedanta Society, 1947).

sense organs. Bow down in devotion to your guru. Then enter the lotus of the heart and there meditate on the presence of Brahman—the pure, the blissful.

"Unmanifest to the senses, beyond all thought, infinite in form, is God. He is the doer of all good; he is forever tranquil; he is immortal. He is One, without beginning, middle, or end; he is all-pervading. He is infinite wisdom, and he is bliss.

"The seers meditate on him and reach the source of all beings, the witness of all. They go beyond all darkness. He is Brahma, he is Shiva, he is Indra, he is the supreme, the changeless Reality. He is Vishnu, he is the primal energy, he is eternity. He is all. He is what has been and what shall be. He who knows him conquers death. There is no other way to liberation."

Now let us consider each of the above ideas separately.

Who lives in solitude.

Narada gives advice to all spiritual aspirants to have the association of the holy, receive the grace of a great soul, and now he says that an aspirant must also live in solitude. This does not mean to live in solitude throughout his life—there is then the danger of becoming self-centered. To live in solitude for some time or even occasionally is very important and necessary for monks as well as for householders. To live in solitude means to devote oneself wholeheartedly to God, away from worldly distractions. As Sri Krishna says in the Bhagavad-Gita:

> Turn all your thought
> Toward solitude, spurning

APHORISM 47

The noise of the crowd,
Its fruitless commotion.

While living in solitude, intensify your longing for
God—meditate, chant the name of the Lord and praise
his glory, study the scriptures and meditate on their
meanings. Thus must you pass your time for some
while in order that love for God may grow.

To quote Sri Ramakrishna in this connection:

"If you want butter, the milk must be curdled and
set in a place where no one can disturb it; otherwise
the curd will not stand. Then churn it and the butter
will rise. Similarly the neophyte should sit in solitude
and not be disturbed by worldly-minded people; then
through the churning of the settled mind by the practice of meditation the butter of divine love will be
acquired. If you give your mind to God in solitude,
you will obtain the spirit of renunciation and absolute
devotion. If you give the mind to the world, it will
grow worldly and think of lust and greed.

"The world may be likened to water, and the mind
to milk. Pure milk once mixed with water cannot be
separated from it; but if it is first turned into butter
and then placed in water, it can remain separate. Let
the milk of your mind be turned into the butter of
divine love by means of religious practice in solitude.
The mind then will never get mixed with the water
of worldliness, but will rise above and remain un-
attached to the world. Having attained true knowledge and devotion, the mind will stand apart from
the world."[1]

Who . . . cuts through the bondages of the world.
"When the milk of the mind has been turned into

1 *Ibid.*

the butter of divine love," it does not become attached to worldliness. Such a man is freed from the bondages of the world. Not that he necessarily runs away from the world or, if he is a householder, runs away from his parents, wife, or children; but he learns to see his family as God's family, and he sees God in each of them and serves them with greater love, for his love for his family then becomes an entirely selfless love.

Who . . . goes beyond the three gunas.

The best commentary on this is to be found in the fourteenth chapter of the Gita, which I will summarize as follows:

Krishna tells Arjuna, his devotee and friend, that the three *gunas* (types of energy) come forth from *prakriti* (primordial nature). They are known as *sattva*, *rajas*, and *tamas*. Sattva expresses itself in purity, clarity, and mental calm; rajas in restlessness, passion, and activity; tamas in ignorance and inertia. In the process of evolution, sattva represents an ideal form which is to be realized; rajas, the force which makes its realization possible; tamas, the inert mass which rajas moves and shapes in order to achieve sattva. The gunas are in a state of constant interaction, and a man's mood changes whenever one guna prevails over the two others.

Krishna points out that all three gunas are bonds which imprison the dweller within the body and prevent him from knowing the Atman, his true nature. Tamas is the bondage of sloth, stupidity, and cowardice. Rajas is the bondage of lust, greed, and compulsive activity. Even sattva binds us, by making us search for happiness and worldly knowledge instead of enlightenment.

Therefore, says Krishna, the wise man must over-come the gunas in order to break his bonds and be-come free. He is to do this by the exercise of discrim-ination. He must not hate the gunas and the moods which are caused by them; he must not identify him-self with the actions they cause him to perform. He must remind himself that it is they who are really the doers of all deeds, not he. He observes them, while remaining apart, at one with the Atman. He regards happiness and suffering, praise and blame, riches and poverty, with an equal eye, never allowing himself to give way to elation or despair. He feels no lack of anything.

Krishna concludes by telling Arjuna: "If a man worships me with unfaltering love, he will go beyond these three gunas."

Who . . . depends upon the Lord even for his living.
The teachings contained in these aphorisms are the highest teachings. A person cannot follow them all at once. One must struggle and practice to think of God more and more, and then, when love for him begins to develop in the heart, the aspirant easily and natural-ly becomes able to follow them.

For instance, who can entirely depend upon the Lord even for his living? Only he who has completely sur-rendered himself to the Lord and who constantly feels his living presence within.

In the Bhagavad-Gita Sri Krishna tells his disciple Arjuna:

"But if a man will worship me, and meditate upon me with an undistracted mind, devoting every moment to me, I shall carry to him everything that he needs, and protect his possessions from loss."

115

There is an interesting legend associated with this verse. There was a great scholar who was a priest. He was writing a commentary on the Bhagavad-Gita. When he came to this particular verse, he was puzzled, for he thought to himself, how would Lord Krishna *carry to* his devotee everything he needs? He concluded that this particular phrase was an interpolation. So he scratched out the phrase *vahamyaham* (I carry) and substituted the phrase *dadamyaham* (I supply).

The scholar worked as a priest in a village some distance from his home. He managed to earn only enough from day to day for himself and his family. (In India priests may marry.) Now it happened that the day he scratched out that particular phrase from the Gita, he went to the distant village to do his priestly duty, and a storm arose which raged all day and night; it was impossible for him to return home. He worried all night that his wife and children would be without food until his return the next day. However, during his absence from home, a young boy carried in a big basket loaded with fruits and groceries and handed it to the wife of the priest, saying, "Your husband cannot return until tomorrow, so he sent this basket which I have carried here for you and the children. But I must tell you, your husband scratched my forehead before he sent me. You can see the marks here." Thus saying, the boy disappeared. When the husband returned home, worried that his wife and children had suffered from hunger, he apologized and said he had been unable to come home because of the raging storm. But his wife said, "Why, you sent a young boy who carried a basket of food for us, and we had a

116

delightful feast. But what's the matter with you that you could be so cruel to that young boy? You scratched his forehead and there were traces of blood." Then suddenly it struck the priest that it was the Lord himself who had carried to them what they needed. So in the edition of the Bhagavad-Gita which he was commenting on, he repeated the phrase *vahamyaham* three times—I carry, I carry, I carry.

48. (Who, indeed, crosses this maya?) *He who gives up the fruits of his actions, renounces all selfish activities, and passes beyond the pairs of opposites.*

It has already been mentioned that the law of karma, the law of cause and effect, works not only in the physical world, but it applies in the moral and mental world as well. The law of karma states that if I do a good deed for you, or if I have a loving thought about you, I will get my reward; whether you yourself give me that reward or not does not matter. If I do good, I shall receive good in return. If I do something bad, bad will come back to me. Our happinesses and miseries are caused by our own actions and thoughts. That is the law.

Freedom or perfection cannot be achieved as long as we are bound by this law of karma. For every action or thought not only produces happiness or misery, according to the nature of our actions and thoughts, but also impressions in our minds and tendencies which cause us to remain subject to birth and death and rebirth.

Freedom from the law of karma does not mean we have to give up action or stop thinking. What is it that causes our bondage to the law of karma? It is our attachment to action and to the fruits of our work. So Narada here teaches us to give up the fruits of work and to renounce all selfish activities.

The secret is taught by Sri Krishna in the Bhagavad-Gita:

"You have the right to work, but for the work's sake only. You have no right to the fruits of work. Desire for the fruits of work must never be your motive in working. Never give way to laziness either.

"Perform every action with your heart fixed on the Supreme Lord. Renounce attachment to the fruits.

"In the calm of self-surrender you can free yourself from the bondage of virtue and vice during this very life. Devote yourself, therefore, to reaching union with Brahman. To unite the heart with Brahman and then to act: that is the secret of non-attached work. In the calm of self-surrender, the seers renounce the fruits of their actions, and so reach enlightenment. Then they are free from the bondage of rebirth, and pass to that state which is beyond all evil."

Thus it is that the devotee's whole life becomes an unending ritual since every action is performed as worship, not in the hope of personal gain or advantage.

To many people, nonattachment suggests indifference, laziness, or fatalism. Actually nonattachment is the very opposite of indifference. It is a positive virtue, born of devotion to God. Through the practice of non-attachment and selfless service the devotee frees himself from the wheel of cause and effect, deed and reward, and obtains the Infinite.

He who . . . passes beyond the pairs of opposites.

Heat and cold, pleasure and pain, success and failure,

and so forth—the pairs of opposites—are experienced as long as we live in this world of the senses.

Sri Krishna teaches in the Bhagavad-Gita:

"A serene spirit accepts pleasure and pain with an even mind, and is unmoved by either. He alone is worthy of immortality.

"Be even-tempered in success and failure; for it is this evenness of temper which is meant by yoga."

But the main question is how to gain this poise in the midst of the opposites of life. My master taught, "Hold on to the pillar of God." (In India children like to hold on to a pillar and swing around it, and as long as they hold on to the pillar, they cannot fall.) If you thus hold to the pillar of God, then even storm and stress will not be able to upset you.

Furthermore, the great secret is to be free from the sense that "I am the doer." But this freedom from the sense of "I and mine" or "I am the doer" is a high state.

However, the more you think of God, the more love for him will grow and your ego will become less and less. So hold to the pillar of God.

49. (Who, indeed, crosses this maya?) *He who renounces even the rites and ceremonies prescribed by the scriptures and attains unfaltering love for God.* (Cf. aphorisms 12, 13, 14.)

We need to follow the injunctions of the scriptures and to practice spiritual disciplines until that supreme love arises in our hearts. This attainment of supreme love, as often pointed out, is identical with attaining the illumined knowledge of God, which means that

119

such a person lives in unending, blissful consciousness. What need then is there to follow the injunctions of the scriptures?

50. *Such a man, indeed, crosses this maya, and helps others to cross it.*

In the preceding three aphorisms, hints for spiritual disciplines have been given.

Let me now quote the words of Sri Krishna in the Bhagavad-Gita, to remind readers what spiritual disciplines an aspirant must undergo:

> Learn from me now,
> O son of Kunti,
> How man made perfect
> Is one with Brahman,
> The goal of wisdom.
> When the mind and the heart
> Are freed from delusion,
> United with Brahman,
> When steady will
> Has subdued the senses,
> When sight and taste
> And sound are abandoned
> Without regretting,
> Without aversion;
> When man seeks solitude,
> Eats but little,
> Curbing his speech,
> His mind and body,
> Ever engaged
> In his meditation

On Brahman the truth,
And full of compassion;
When he casts from him
Vanity, violence,
Pride, lust, anger
And all his possessions,
Totally free
From the sense of ego
And tranquil of heart:
That man is ready
For oneness with Brahman.
And he who dwells
United with Brahman,
Calm in mind,
Not grieving, not craving,
Regarding all men
With equal acceptance:
He loves me most dearly.

If a devotee follows those disciplines, he attains supreme love and lives in a state of constant illumination.
The illumined heart is liberated from the bondage of
maya. Such a man alone experiences eternal joy. He
becomes a true guru who helps others also to be liberated from the bondage of maya.

In aphorisms 39-42, which have been explained, Narada stresses the need of a guru, pointing out how
through his grace a man attains liberation from the
bondages of maya.

In this connection, I must also point out that such
great illumined souls "purify the whole world," as Sri
Krishna says in the Srimad Bhagavatam. Once my master told me about Swami Premananda, his brother dis-

121

ciple: "Do you know what a great soul he is, what holiness he emanates? In whichever direction his eyes look that whole direction becomes purified." After the many years since their passing away, whenever I think of these disciples of Sri Ramakrishna, I feel purified and can breathe holiness.

The fact is that the illumined souls do not necessarily have to talk or preach. Thoughts are contagious, holiness is contagious. Even if a holy man shuts himself in a room, his life, his holiness, his love for God will help all mankind; this help comes to those who open their hearts to receive the grace of God, who aspire to spiritual attainment. Thoughts of purity and holiness are in the atmosphere; Christ, Krishna, Buddha, Ramakrishna, and other great holy men and women, though not living in physical bodies, are still helping and guiding mankind.

VII

PREPARATORY AND SUPREME DEVOTION

51. *The real nature of this supreme love is inexpressible.*

52. *It is like a dumb man trying to express his experience of a delightful taste.*

As has been explained in commenting on aphorisms 15 and 30, it is impossible to express in words the experience of this supreme love, which is realized in the state of nirvikalpa samadhi.

Once the disciples of Sri Ramakrishna urged the Master to describe this supreme experience, and when he made the attempt, he immediately went into samadhi. Every time that he sought to express it in words he would have the experience itself, and there would be complete silence.

Sri Ramakrishna used to say that it is like a salt doll wanting to measure the depth of the ocean. The salt doll wanted to tell others how deep the water was, but as soon as it got into the ocean it melted. Then how could it report on the depth of the water?

Narada gives the example of a dumb man's experience of a delightful taste, which he cannot describe in words. Similarly this experience of supreme love for God is only to be felt within one's self and cannot be expressed in words.

PREPARATORY AND SUPREME DEVOTION

There is a story in the Upanishads of a young man who was sent by his father to learn the knowledge of Brahman. The first time he came back and was asked by his father what he had learned, he gave a fine discourse on the nature of Brahman. The father of the boy then told him to go back and learn some more. The second time he came back and was asked the same question by his father; the boy remained silent. Then the father exclaimed, "Why, my boy, your face shines like a knower of Brahman. You have experienced him. His name is Silence."

Sri Ramakrishna gives the illustration of a bee making a big noise until it sits on a flower. As it sits on the flower and sucks the honey it becomes silent. Again sometimes, when it has become drunk by drinking deep of the honey, it makes a sweet humming noise. Similarly after drinking deep of God's love and becoming God-intoxicated, some speak of the Lord in many ways —but they can never express their inner experiences.

53.   (Though it is inexpressible), *nevertheless, it is manifest in the great souls who have attained it.*

It is true that this experience of supreme love, the experience of unitary consciousness realized by the great ones, is inexpressible in words, but nevertheless, their exemplary lives are guideposts to spiritual aspirants. The aspirants can feel in the company of these free souls how they live in a state of blissful consciousness, and how their love flows toward all beings. In the presence of my own master, all of us felt a current of joy within ourselves, and he made us see how simple

124

and easy it is to realize God. God is like a fruit we are holding in the palms of our own hands. He would make us feel that God is nearer than the nearest, dearer than the dearest. Thus it is that these great ones can communicate in silence the truth of God to the aspirants.

There is a pen picture drawn by Shankara. The master is sitting silently under a tree, he is young; the disciples are sitting round him, they are old; they are also silent. Gradually the disciples' doubts are dissolved, and the Truth is revealed to them.

The master is young, because the truth of God is ever new and eternal. The disciples are old, because superstitions and ignorance have existed from a beginningless time.

54. *This supreme love is devoid of attributes; it is free from all selfish desires; it grows in intensity every moment; it is an unbroken inner experience, subtler than the subtlest.*

This supreme love is the real nature of the Atman or Brahman; that is to say, Brahman or God is love itself—hence devoid of attributes. When this love arises in a man's heart, he realizes his oneness with God, who is love itself. In ordinary human love, love arises because the lover sees certain attributes or qualities in the beloved. But in this divine love, love knows no reason except that love is its own fruit.

When a man attains this love, he has found the treasure of all treasures, and there is a complete fulfillment. All selfish desires appear then as mere beads of glass.

PREPARATORY AND SUPREME DEVOTION

Sarada Devi, the Holy Mother, used to teach us to pray that we may be desireless so that we can find fulfillment in our complete union with God.

In the great souls, however, there is one desire left, if it can be called a desire. The heart of a great soul is full of compassion, and so his one desire is that all mankind may find this love which brings the "peace that passeth understanding."

This supreme love grows in intensity every moment and is ever new. My master used to say, "Light, more light, more light! Is there any end to it?"

There is an interesting legend about a devotee of Shiva. In India one sees the image of a bull in front of the image of Shiva. The bull, so the legend goes, represents a great devotee of Lord Shiva, whose love grew to such intensity, and who experienced such ecstatic joy, that his human frame could hold it no longer. So he was transformed into a strong bull in order that he could hold that intense love and joy and remain calm.

It is an unbroken inner experience, subtler than the subtlest.

A bhakta remains immersed in the bliss and sweetness continuously. Once a young aspirant asked Swami Turiyananda, "Swami, do you not sleep?" He answered, "Yes, I sleep; but my sleep is not like yours." That is to say, even in sleep he experienced that inner joy. It is subtler than the subtlest, because it can only be felt and cannot be expressed in words. It is inexpressible and indescribable, because this experience is the experience of Sat-chit-ananda Brahman—the absolute Existence, pure Consciousness, and Love itself.

55. *When a man attains this supreme love, he sees his Beloved everywhere, he hears of him everywhere, he talks only of him, and he thinks of him only.*

In fact he is continually united with his beloved Lord. He receives the divine sight, and he sees nothing but Brahman. Behind this apparent universe of multiplicity, he sees the one Reality. Such a man regards with an equal eye all beings and creatures.

As a matter of fact, we are really perceiving Brahman all the time, only the universe of name and form is superimposed upon him. Indeed this universe is nothing but Brahman; but because we are under the spell of maya, we are not aware of it. Until the divine sight is opened, we see only matter and physical objects with our physical eyes. With the eye of the Spirit, the enlightened man sees Brahman everywhere under all circumstances.

He hears of him everywhere.

Any sound that he hears reminds him only of God's word. Sri Ramakrishna, in a state of ecstasy, said, "O Mother, Thou art the sound of all the letters in the alphabet. Thou art in the scriptures as well as in what may sound improper or indecent. Thou art in all those sounds." Uttering these words, Sri Ramakrishna went into samadhi.

The illumined heart sees behind the veil of good and evil the single light of his Beloved.

He talks only of him, and he thinks of him only.

Shankara says:

"How could a wise man reject the experience of supreme bliss and take delight in mere outward form?

127

When the moon shines in its exceeding beauty, who would care to look at a painted moon?"

Then he teaches us how to live our lives in God:

"Experience of the unreal offers us no satisfaction, nor any escape from misery. Find satisfaction, therefore, in the experience of the sweet bliss of Brahman. Devote yourself to the Atman and live happily forever.

"O noble soul, this is how you must pass your days—see the Atman everywhere, enjoy the bliss of the Atman, fix your thought upon the Atman, the one without a second."

56. *Preparatory devotion is of three kinds, according to the predominance in the minds of the aspirants of one or another of the three gunas—sattva, rajas, and tamas; also according to the reasons for which they devote themselves to God—whether because they are world-weary, or seeking for knowledge, or desirous of the fulfillment of some material desires.*

In some of the preceding aphorisms the nature of supreme love has been discussed. Summarily it can be stated that when a bhakta through the grace of his guru and of God attains to supreme love and is illumined by the knowledge of God, he transcends the three gunas, he is free from selfish desires, he sees his Beloved everywhere, and he has an unbroken inner experience of bliss in God.

This is a state to be experienced through the practice of spiritual disciplines. Of course there are some exceptional souls who are born with this supreme love; they are forever pure and free. The avatars are born with such knowledge and devotion, as are those who are known as *Ishvarakotis*—these are found among the disciples of an avatar. But ordinary people have to struggle hard to attain that devotion and knowledge.

Bhakti, or devotion, may, as already stated, mean the preparatory devotion and also the attainment. In this particular aphorism it is explained again that there are different classes of people who practice devotion according to their different natures and tendencies. I have already discussed in aphorism 1, how there are different classes of people who devote themselves to God—the world-weary, the seekers for knowledge, or those who have unfulfilled desires and seek for God's help. Lastly, in that connection, I mentioned the wise, who are discriminative. These are described by Sri Krishna. They know the vanity of everything and they love God for love's sake. They are the highest class, and Sri Krishna says of them, "They are my very Self." Such devotees are nearest to attaining the supreme love and enlightenment.

In aphorism 56, the division is also made according to the predominance of one or another of the gunas—sattva, rajas, and tamas.

The sattvic devotee devotes himself to God; his one ideal is to be free from the bondages of worldliness and to reach union with God. His heart's one prayer is to have pure love for God and pure knowledge of him.

The rajasic devotee devotes himself to God for the sake of such material ends as success, health, and prosperity.

The tamasic devotee, like the rajasic devotee, has not yet reached the stage of discrimination between the eternal and noneternal. The tamasic devotee is religious in the ordinary sense of the word; that is to say, his is a Sunday religion. He attends church regularly, puts money in the collection basket, prays a little, and sings the glory of God in the choir. The goal of life is not yet clearly defined or understood by him.

But we must remember that tamasic devotion is a step toward reaching the stage of a rajasic devotee. Finally the devotee reaches the stage of sattva.

It does not matter how one begins to devote oneself to God. Even a little prayer, a little thought of God leads us gradually to the supreme attainment.

Sri Ramakrishna used to classify devotees into three divisions. Devotees of the highest class see the Beloved everywhere; the manifold universe is but many forms of God, or God appearing in so many masks. They see God in Brahma, the Creator of the universe, as well as in a blade of grass. Devotees of the middle class see God within the shrine of their own hearts and know him to be the inner ruler, the witness. Devotees of the lowest class look toward the sky and say, "God is up there."

57. *Of these classes of devotees, the first is considered the highest, after these come the less high, the middling, and the low.*

We must once more state that they all ultimately reach the transcendental or supreme love. Begin to devote yourself to God—no matter for what reason. You have taken the first step toward him then.

VIII

THE FORMS OF DIVINE LOVE

58. *The path of devotion is the easiest way to attain God.*

The path of devotion is easiest, because everyone has love in his heart. It is something indefinable, but is felt and experienced in one's own heart. Parents love their children, children love the parents; there is conjugal love, and love among friends. Whichever form love may take, its very nature is divine. The attraction that we feel for one another is the attraction of God dwelling in everyone, but we are not aware of it. So the path of devotion is a way that anyone can follow easily, if only he directs his love knowingly toward God. There is a beautiful prayer by a great sage, Prahlada: "Lord, may I attain that love for you that the worldly people have for the objects of the world." Love finds its fulfillment only when we turn this love toward the one Reality, whose very nature is love. As you approach nearer and nearer to God, you will begin to feel his love in the same way that you feel the cool breeze of the ocean on a hot day as you come nearer to the ocean.

And as you begin to feel God's love, your love for him grows in intensity. Then it is that you learn to love God with all your heart, soul, mind, and strength, and you attain the vision of God in the lower form of samadhi. Ultimately you attain the highest samadhi and reach your union with God. "Not I but Thou.

131

The old man is gone; only Thou remainest. I am Thou."

59. *Love is its own proof and does not require any other.*

60. *Its nature is peace and supreme bliss.*

Love is felt and experienced in one's own heart. That itself is its own validity.

The nature of this divine love, which is peace and supreme bliss, is only experienced when a man has reached his union with God. One may find peace and joy in human love, but they are not lasting. The peace and joy that you experience through devotion to God is lasting and continuous, and it grows in intensity.

61. *The devotee does not grieve at any personal loss, for he has surrendered himself, everything he has, and even the rites and ceremonies which are enjoined by the scriptures.*

In fact, the devotee does not feel that he owns anything of this world. He has completely surrendered himself to the Lord. Self-surrender, as already explained by Narada, is the culmination of spiritual life. All spiritual disciplines are undertaken in order that we can surrender ourselves to God and his will. My only refuge art Thou, O Lord. I am Thine, I am Thine; Thou art my own, my very own. Thus it is that the heart of a devotee is ever filled with love for God. Profit or loss does not enter into his mind.

His heart is ever filled with the bliss of God. Rites

and ceremonies as enjoined by the scriptures become
no longer necessary to him. As Sri Ramakrishna used
to say, *sandhya* (the regular rites which a brahmin
performs three times a day) merges in *Gayatri* (a
Vedic prayer which a brahmin repeats daily). Gayatri
ends in the simple utterance of the sacred syllable Om,
and Om merges into Silence.

62. *Even though the devotee may have surrendered*
    himself utterly to the Lord, he must not renounce
    action in the world but continue to perform it,
    giving up the fruits of action to the Lord.

Take, for instance, the lives of great teachers like
Krishna, Buddha, Christ, or Ramakrishna. They had
realized God; they became one with God. Their vision
changed. They saw the one God, the one blissful Consciousness, pervading everywhere. Yet we find them
teaching and preaching. They came down from the
highest experience, and their hearts went out to those
who were weary and heavy-laden and knew not God.
They taught for the good of mankind living in ignorance.

As Sri Krishna says in the Bhagavad-Gita: "Consider
me: I am not bound by any sort of duty. There is
nothing, in all the three worlds, which I do not already
possess; nothing I have yet to acquire. But I go on
working, nevertheless. If I did not continue to work
untiringly as I do, mankind would still follow me, no
matter where I led them. Suppose I were to stop? They
would all be lost."

My master, Maharaj, once told me: "I see God playing and wearing so many masks, the mask of a saint,

133

the mask of a sinner, the mask of an honest man, the mask of a thief. How then can I teach anybody? But I come down from that experience, and then I see your mistakes and try to correct you."

Sri Ramakrishna used to say that the great illumined souls retain the "ego of knowledge" in order to teach mankind. This ego has touched the philosopher's stone, as it were, and it has turned into gold and can do no harm.

63. *Conversations about lust, greed, and atheism should not be listened to.*

In this and the following three aphorisms, Narada is telling us what we must avoid in order to attain to supreme love. In one of the preceding aphorisms he has advised us to shun evil company. Here he tells us that we should not only avoid the company of the lustful, the greedy, and the godless, but avoid even listening to talk about them. This teaching is meant particularly for the beginners in spiritual life.

64. *Pride, vanity, and such other vices must be cast out.*

Swami Vivekananda defined religion as the "unfoldment of the divinity already within man." Perfection or divinity is the true nature of every being. It exists potentially in every man, but it is shut in by the locks and bars of ignorance. What is the nature of this ignorance? First it hides the indwelling God—the absolute Existence, pure blissful Consciousness, and abiding Love. Next it creates the sense of ego. This ego is created by identification of the pure indwelling God with the mind, senses, body, and so forth. From this sense of ego again arise attachment to the objects and persons who give us pleasure, and aversion to things and persons who give us pain or suffering. Sri Krishna says in the Bhagavad-Gita: "The attraction and aversion which the senses feel for different objects are natural. But you must not give way to such feelings; they are obstacles." Also there arises the desire to cling to this surface life. To quote the words of Christ: "For whosoever will save his life shall lose it." Behind or underneath this surface life there is the eternal life in God.

This does not mean, however, that we must not love people, or that we must be indifferent to the objects of the world and desist from activities in the world.

Furthermore, Sri Krishna says:

When he has no lust, no hatred,
A man walks safely among the things of lust
    and hatred.
To obey the Atman
Is his peaceful joy:
Sorrow melts
Into that clear peace:
His quiet mind
Is soon established in peace.

The uncontrolled mind
Does not guess that the Atman is present:
How can it meditate?
Without meditation, where is peace?
Without peace, where is happiness?

Egotism causes the mind to become restless and un-

135

controlled. From egotism also arise pride, vanity, and desire for name and fame. All these are the greatest obstacles to the removal of ignorance.

There is a verse in Sanskrit: "Pride is like an intoxicant drink, honor is the filth of a pig, and fame is the worst kind of hell. O man, shun these three evils and be happy!"

Swami Vivekananda had experienced the greatest fame and received the greatest honor, both in India and the West. Swami Ambikananda, a disciple of Maharaj, who knew Swamiji intimately, wrote to me that he had seen Swamiji in a state of ecstasy, unconscious of his surroundings, walking up and down the grounds of the Belur Monastery and chanting the above verse again and again.

The sense of ego, however, is not all bad. As has already been said, the great illumined souls keep their ego of knowledge in order to teach mankind. A spiritual aspirant has to have an ego in order that he can ultimately transcend it. So for him also there is the ego of knowledge, which makes him long for God and want to love God. He must feel that he is a child of God; he is a servant of God. In short, the ego that separates us from God and from others, the ego that is vain, envious, jealous, the ego that is self-seeking, is the "ego of ignorance." That ego is to be overcome by aspiring to realize God. (See aphorism 27.)

65. *Dedicate all your actions to God and direct all your passions, such as lust, anger, pride, and so forth, toward God.*

There is a ceremony performed, called *homa*, in

which Brahman and *Shakti*, Brahman's power, are invoked into a fire. Oblations are offered and prayers are chanted with the firm conviction that Brahman and its power are present in the fire itself. At the end of the ceremony, all actions with their effects, good or bad, are dedicated to God with the following prayer:

"I, who am an embodied being, endowed with intellect, life-breath, and their functions, now offer up all my actions and their fruits to the fire of Brahman. No matter what I may have done, said, or thought, in waking, in dreaming, or in dreamless sleep, with my mind, my tongue, my hands, or my other members—may all this be an offering to Brahman."

An aspirant should make it his daily practice to offer up mentally all his actions and their fruits to God. Such a practice will purify the heart, and gradually the aspirant will desist from actions which would obstruct his vision of God. Faith and love will grow in his heart.

The passions are present in every one of us. The great teachers often instruct the aspirants to direct the passions to God. In the Srimad Bhagavatam we read: "Whoever directs his lust, anger or other passions towards the Lord with a feeling of identity with Him and devotion to Him is transformed into His Being."

Once, when Swami Turiyananda was a young boy, he approached his master, Sri Ramakrishna, and appealed to him to help him become free from lust. Sri Ramakrishna replied, "Why do you want to be freed from lust? Rather increase your lust." Then the disciple fully understood that to increase lust meant to lust for God and give one's whole heart to Him.

Anger can be directed toward God in this spirit, "O Lord, why won't you reveal yourself to me? How cruel

137

you must be! I am helpless; my heart is dry. Why don't you reveal your grace to me and grant me steadfast love for you!" Or anger can be directed toward the obstacles on our path which prevent us from attaining devotion. Anger will then cease, and dispassion will arise in the heart.

To become proud thinking that you are the child of the Lord, that you are his servant, will gradually make you aware of God, and eventually this pride will wear out and your ego will be merged in the Lord.

Thus it is that when passions are turned toward God, they become aids to acquiring love for God.

66. *Transcending the three forms of love, love the Lord, and love him as his eternal servant, as his eternal bride.*

There are three forms of love through which one may prepare oneself for the attainment of supreme love. From one point of view, these three forms are classified as follows:

(1) A man may devote himself to God because he feels distressed or world-weary.

(2) He may devote himself to God because he has unfulfilled earthly desires and prays for their fulfillment.

(3) He may be a seeker for knowledge.

The supreme love, however, is only attained after he has transcended these three and has spiritual discrimination. Knowing that the one eternal treasure of his heart is God, realizing all is vanity except to love God, he thus becomes devoted to Him. (See aphorism 1.)

In another aspect these three forms are classified as follows: (1) the love of a sattvic devotee, (2) the love of a rajasic devotee, (3) the love of a tamasic devotee.

To attain supreme love a man needs to transcend these three gunas: sattva, rajas, and tamas. (See aphorism 56.)

Sri Krishna describes in the Bhagavad-Gita how by transcending the gunas a man can reach oneness with God. (See aphorism 47.)

Language is inadequate to express this supreme, transcendental, ecstatic love. Nevertheless, the followers of all religions, in all countries, have had to use our inadequate human language to express that divine love. Indeed, human love itself, in its various forms, has been used by the sages as a metaphor to represent this inexpressible divine love. We find them making use of all the terms associated with human love in its many forms to describe their love for God. The lovers of God try to experience this divine love in as many different ways as there are different forms of human love.

There are five types of love in our relationship to God. The first kind is known as *shanta* (peaceful). There is not yet that fire of love, that madness in love, that intensity and longing for God. The devotee still looks upon God with reverence, as all-powerful. His attitude is calm, gentle, and peaceful. This is only the beginning.

The next type is *dasya,* in which the devotee considers himself a servant of the Lord, his child, his very own. In Christianity, we find that this relationship is practiced by the great majority of devotees. It is the ideal of the Fatherhood of God and the brotherhood of man.

139

According to Narada, this relationship gradually brings us closer to God, to an intimacy with him, until God is no longer thought of as almighty, and we no longer consider his greatness and his glories. We come to think of him only as loving and sweet, even more so than our own father.

In this prayer of Sri Chaitanya the Lord is addressed as the "Sweet One."

> A drowning man in this world's fearful ocean
> Is Thy servant, O Sweet One,
> In Thy mercy
> Consider him as dust beneath Thy feet.

The next type of love is *sakhya*, friendship. "Thou art our beloved friend." The shepherd boys of Brindavan are examples of this relationship. Krishna is their beloved friend. They play with him and dance with him.

A man opens his heart to his friend, and he will not chide him for his faults but will always want to help him. Friends are equals, and so equal love flows in and out between the devotee and his friend, God. God becomes the friend to whom we can reveal the innermost secrets of our hearts. He is looked upon as our eternal playmate.

In the Gospel according to St. John we read: "Ye are my friends, if ye do whatsoever I command you.

"Henceforth I call you not servants; for the servant knoweth not what his lord doeth: but I have called you friends; for all things that I have heard of my Father I have made known unto you."

Sri Ramakrishna saw in his mystic vision that Maharaj, my master, was a shepherd boy, dancing with Sri Krishna on a full-blown lotus. Maharaj himself did not know this until the last moment of his life. Just before he passed away, he became aware of it in a mystic vision and exclaimed: "Ah, the blissful ocean of Brahman! Om! Salutations to the Supreme Brahman! Om! Salutations to the Supreme Atman!"

While speaking of these divine experiences, his throat became dry. A disciple offered him a drink, saying, "Maharaj, please drink this water. . . ."

"The mind doesn't want to come down from Brahman," said Maharaj slowly. "Pour Brahman into Brahman," and like a child, he opened his mouth for the water to be poured into it.

Then he turned to Swami Saradananda, a brother-disciple, and said, "Sri Ramakrishna is real. His divine incarnation is real."

After this Maharaj was silent for a while. He was deeply absorbed in meditation, and his face wore an expression of great sweetness. The minds of those who were present were so uplifted that they felt no grief— only joy and silent calm. All sense of the world and of death was lost.

Suddenly, out of the silence, the voice of Maharaj was heard: "Ah, that inexpressible light! Ramakrishna, the Krishna of my Ramakrishna. . . . I am the shepherd boy. Put anklets on my feet, I want to dance with my Krishna. I want to hold his hand—the little boy Krishna. . . . Ah, Krishna, my Krishna, you have come! Krishna, Krishna. . . . Can't you see him? Haven't you eyes to see? Oh, how beautiful! My Krishna—on the lotus—eternal—the Sweet One!

"My play is over now. Look! The boy Krishna is

caressing me. He is calling me to come away with him! I am coming."

Thus to Maharaj, Krishna was the eternal companion and friend.

The next type of love is *vatsalya*, in which the devotee loves God as his child. By taking the attitude of a father or mother of God, we lose our awareness of His power and the feelings of awe, reverence, and obedience, which keep us at a distance from Him. The lover of God does not care to think of Him as almighty, glorious, the Lord of the universe, and so forth. He only wants to love God because He is the Sweet One. He seeks no favor from Him. Of course, this relationship is only possible for those who believe in avatars, a belief which we find among the Hindus and Christians. Many Hindus love Krishna as a baby, known as Gopala; and a Christian may choose to love Christ as baby Jesus.

The Srimad Bhagavatam describes the relationship between the baby Krishna and his foster-mother Yasoda:

"One day when Krishna was still a little baby, some boys saw him eating mud. When his foster mother, Yasoda, learned of it, she asked the baby to open his mouth. Krishna opened his tiny mouth, and wonder of wonders! Yasoda saw the whole universe—earth and heaven, the stars, the planets, the sun and the moon, and innumerable beings—within the mouth of Baby Krishna. For a moment Yasoda was bewildered, thinking, 'Is this a dream or a hallucination? Or is it a real vision, the vision of my little baby as God himself?' Soon she composed herself and prayed to the Lord of Love:

" 'May Thou who hast brought us into this world of maya, may thou who hast given me this sense and consciousness that I am Yasoda, queen of Nanda, the mother of Krishna, bestow thy blessings upon us always.'

"Looking at her baby, she saw him smiling. Then she clasped him to her bosom and kissed him. Yasoda saw him as her own little baby Krishna—him verily who was and is worshiped as the Brahman in Vedanta, as the universal Self in Yoga, and as the God of Love by devotees; and she found an indescribable joy and happiness in her heart whenever she looked upon him."

Many women in India throughout the ages have looked upon themselves as Krishna's mother. The outstanding example in the present age was a woman disciple of Sri Ramakrishna, who became well known as "Gopaler Ma." Sister Nivedita (Margaret Noble), a disciple of Swamiji, who associated intimately with Gopaler Ma, and who retold the stories of her visions of God as Gopala, writes:

"Gopal's Mother was an old woman. She had already been old, fifteen or twenty years before, when she had first walked over, one day at noon from her cell at Kamarhatty by the Ganges-side to see the Master in the garden at Dakshineswar. He received her, so they say, standing at his door, as if he expected her. And she, whose chosen worship had been for many years Gopala, the Babe Krishna, the Christ-child of Hinduism, saw him revealed to her, as in a vision, as she drew near. How true she always was to this! Never once through all the years that followed, did she offer salutations to Sri Ramakrishna, who took her thenceforth as his mother. And never have I known her to speak of our Holy Mother, save as 'my daughter-in-law.' "

THE FORMS OF DIVINE LOVE

There is one more human representation of divine love. It is known as *kanta* or *madhura*—sweet—the Lord is the Beloved. This is based on the highest expression of love in this world, and it is the strongest tie of love known among mankind. In this sweet representation of divine love, God is our husband. We are all women. There is but one man, and that is He, our Beloved.

There is a story of a woman saint, Mirabai, who loved Krishna as her husband. She was a queen, married to a Rajput king but she renounced her husband and kingdom and went to Brindavan. At that time, another saint, a disciple of Sri Chaitanya, lived in Brindavan. Mirabai wished to visit the holy man. But the saint first refused, saying that he did not want to see any woman. To that reply, Mirabai retorted saying that she did not know that any man lived in Brindavan except Sri Krishna, her Beloved. Hearing this, the holy man came running to meet this great saint Mirabai.

The love of the gopis, the shepherdesses, for Krishna is a well-known example of this sweet relationship. (See aphorisms 21, 22.) Speaking of them, Swamiji says:

"When the madness of love comes in your brain, when you understand the blessed gopis, then you will understand what love is. When the whole world will vanish, when all other considerations will have died out, when you will become pure-hearted with no other aim, not even the search for truth, then and then alone will come to you the madness of that love, the strength and the power of that infinite love which the gopis had, that love for love's sake. That is the goal. When you have got that you have got everything."

We must remember in this connection that although the pleasure derived from gratification of the sex-urge is regarded as the supreme experience in the sense-world, it is but trivial and momentary. Sri Rama-krishna tells us that the bliss derived from loving God as the Beloved is so intense that it is like sex-pleasure experienced through every single pore of the body; and that this bliss is eternal and infinite.

Sri Ramakrishna, who was the embodiment of purity, had experienced this sweet relationship, and whenever he would think of it, or mention it, he would immediately be absorbed in the bliss of samadhi.

To quote from the Gospel of Sri Ramakrishna: " 'I see everything like a man with jaundiced eyes! I see Thee alone everywhere. O Krishna, Friend of the lowly! O Eternal Consort of my soul! O Govinda!'

"As he uttered the words 'Eternal Consort of my soul' and 'Govinda,' the Master became absorbed in samadhi."

Other great mystics of the world have experienced their oneness with the Beloved. In the words of Plotinus:

"Often when I awake out of bodily slumber and come to a realizing sense of myself I retire from the world outside and give myself up to inward contemplation. Then I behold a wonderful Beauty; I believe that I really belong to a higher and better world, and still I develop within me a glorious life and become one with Godhead. And by this means, I receive such energy of life that I rise above all other things of even the intelligible world; what then must he experience who now beholds the Absolute Beauty in and for itself in all its purity, without corporeal shape, freed from all bondage to space and time! And this, therefore, is the life of the gods and of divine and happy men, a liberation from all earthly concerns, a life unaccompanied by human pleasure, and there is the flight of the alone to the Alone."

In the "Song of Solomon" we find divine love described in its aspect as the "sweet" relationship:

"Let him kiss me with the kisses of his mouth: for thy love is better than wine.

"Because of the savour of thy good ointments thy name *is as* ointment poured forth, therefore do the virgins love thee."

In "The Dark Night," a poem by St. John of the Cross, we read how the lover is brought to the Beloved, and how a mystic marriage takes place:

> Upon my flowery breast
> Wholly for Him and save Himself for none,
> There did I give sweet rest
> To my beloved one.

Could it be that John the Baptist had the same relationship in mind when he spoke of Christ?

"He that hath the bride is the bridegroom: but the friend of the bridegroom, which standeth and heareth him, rejoiceth greatly because of the bridegroom's voice: this my joy therefore is fulfilled."

These are the different aspects of divine love represented in human terms and in human language. But in reality, when love for God arises in the heart in any aspect, that love is overwhelming and so intense that the devotee forgets this world and forgets all earthly ties.

In the words of Vivekananda:

"All the different kinds of love which we see in the world, and with which we are more or less playing merely, have God as the one goal: but unfortunately, man does not know the infinite ocean into which this mighty river of love is constantly flowing, and so, foolishly, he often tries to direct it to little dolls of human beings. The tremendous love for the child that is in human nature is not for the little doll of a child; if you bestow it blindly and exclusively on the child, you will suffer in consequence. But through such suffering will come the awakening by which you are sure to find out that the love which is in you, if it is given to any human being, will sooner or later bring pain and sorrow as the result. Our love must therefore be given to the Highest One, who never dies and never changes, to Him in the ocean of whose love there is neither ebb nor tide. Love must get to its right destination, it must go unto Him who is really the infinite ocean of love. All rivers flow into the ocean. Even the drop of water coming down from the mountain-side cannot stop its course after reaching a brook or a river, however big it may be; at last even that drop somehow does find its way to the ocean. God is the one goal of all our passions and emotions."

The author of the *Cloud of Unknowing* has truly said:

"By Love may He be gotten and holden but by thought never."

67. *The highest class of devotees are those who have one-pointed love for God, and for love's sake only.*

In the Srimad Bhagavatam, Sri Krishna says to his disciple Uddhava:

147

"To the man who finds delight in me alone, who is self-controlled and even-minded, having no longing in his heart but for me, the whole universe is full of bliss. Neither the position of Brahma nor that of Indra, neither domination over the whole world, nor occult power, nor even salvation, is desired by the devotee who has surrendered himself unto me and who finds bliss in me."

This indeed is transcendental love. The great commandment in the Bible describes it also:

"Thou shalt love the Lord thy God with all thy heart, and with all thy soul, and with all thy mind."

If a man establishes one or another of these relationships with God, turning all his thoughts day and night lovingly toward Him, seeking Him and Him only with intense longing in his heart, he will soon find the grace of the Lord and realize God's overwhelming love for mankind. He may then be considered to belong to the highest class of devotees.

The Lord dwells in the hearts of all. Who then is his devotee? He who dwells in Him with his whole soul, heart, and mind. Such a devotee not only sees God in his own heart and realizes his oneness with Him, but he sees the same Lord in the hearts of all, and serves God in all mankind, knowing His oneness with all. "Love your neighbour as yourself," because your neighbor is your self.

68. *When devotees talk of God, their voices choke, tears flow from their eyes, their hair stands erect in ecstasy. Such men as these purify not only*

*their families but this whole earth on which they
are born.*

In the Gospel according to St. Matthew we read:
"For where two or three are gathered together in my
name, there am I in the midst of them."

Suppose you enter into a darkened chamber where
your beloved is lying. You touch the wall, the fur-
niture, the bed, and you know you have not yet found
him. Then you suddenly touch his feet, his limbs, you
know this is he. He talks with you and you are in
his embrace. Thus it is when you first have the vision
of God. But that is not enough. As you talk with God,
you begin to feel intimacy with him, and there arise
in your heart ecstatic love and bliss that are inexpressible. At last you realize your oneness with him.
But then again you separate yourself from him in
order to enjoy his company perpetually. And you
seek company of other devotees of God.

In the life of Sri Ramakrishna we read how he
lived in a constant vision of God the Mother; yet he
would long for the companionship of the devotees.
Often he would say pleadingly: "O Mother, wait a
little. Let me enjoy the company of your devotees."

My master told me how he saw Sri Ramakrishna
become absorbed in samadhi many times during the
day and night, while conversing with the devotees.
Sri Ramakrishna was unique in this respect. Rare
indeed are those who have become absorbed in that
highest samadhi even once in their lives.

The Bhagavad-Gita speaks of the joy which devotees
experience when they are together:

149

Mind and sense are absorbed, I alone am the
theme of their discourse:
Thus delighting each other, they live in bliss
and contentment.
Always aware of the Lord are they, and ever
devoted:
Therefore the strength of their thought is
illumined and guided towards me.

Sri Rama said to his brother Lakshmana, "Wherever you see a devotee weeping and dancing in my name, know that I am manifest there." This weeping and dancing in the name of the Lord is caused by the ecstatic joy that arises in the heart of a devotee. Sri Chaitanya describes it in a prayer:

Ah, how I long for the day
When in chanting Thy name, the tears will
spill down
From my eyes, and my throat will refuse to
utter
Its prayers, choking and stammering with ecstasy,
When all the hairs of my body will stand erect
with joy!

In the Sutasamhita we read: "The whole family is purified, the mother becomes blessed, the earth is rendered pure by a devotee whose heart and mind are absorbed in the boundless ocean of Existence-Knowledge-Bliss."

The greater the devotee, the wider is the sphere of his spiritual influence. Maharaj created a sphere of spirituality around him wherever he went. Whoever came near him would become purified and transformed. Wherever he was, those around him would feel that they were taking part in an unending festival of joy. It is such great mystics who are the light of the world.

Sri Krishna says to his disciple Uddhava in the Srimad Bhagavatam:

"He who loves me is made pure; his heart melts in joy. He rises to transcendental consciousness by the rousing of his higher emotional nature. Tears of joy flow from his eyes; his hair stands on end; his heart melts in love. The bliss in that state is so intense that forgetful of himself and his surroundings he sometimes weeps profusely, or laughs, or sings, or dances; such a devotee is a purifying influence upon the whole universe."

69. *These great illumined souls, the lovers of God, sanctify the places of pilgrimage. The deeds they perform become examples of good action. They give spiritual authority to the scriptures.*

In every country, the birthplaces of great souls are considered as places of pilgrimage. For centuries many spiritual aspirants have practiced disciplines and found enlightenment by residing in such places. Then, later, other illumined souls visit these places, go into samadhi and have ecstatic experiences of God, thereby creating an even more intense spiritual atmosphere and further sanctifying them. I shall cite some examples of how this has happened in recent times.

At Madura, in southern India, there is a famous temple dedicated to the Divine Mother. When my master, Maharaj, entered it and stood before the deity, he exclaimed: "Mother! Mother!" and lost his external consciousness. Swami Ramakrishnananda, who was with him, saw his condition and held him by the arms to prevent him from falling. Seeing Maharaj standing unconscious in ecstasy, the priests and devotees who were present gazed at him in silence. An intense stillness pervaded the temple crowded with pilgrims, and lasted for more than an hour. When Maharaj regained his normal consciousness, he went silently away. Later he described his vision of the luminous form of Divine Mother.

At the temple of Rameswar, dedicated to Lord Shiva, Maharaj became absorbed in samadhi. Even after he had returned to normal consciousness, he remained for some time in a state of ecstatic joy.

Many times in the different holy places he had such ecstatic experiences.

Swami Saradananda, a disciple of Sri Ramakrishna, visited St. Peter's church in Rome. As he entered the church, he went into samadhi. Afterward he simply stated that St. Peter's church was originally built as a wooden frame building, which he saw in his vision.

Swami Vijnanananda, another disciple of Sri Ramakrishna, once told me about one of his spiritual experiences. I recorded his words at the time.

"I went to visit Sarnath. [Sarnath is located near Benares; it is the place where Buddha, after attaining enlightenment, preached his first sermon.] Suddenly I lost all physical consciousness, my mind seemed almost to have vanished. I was enveloped in an Ocean of Light, the Light that is vibrant with peace, joy, and consciousness. I felt as if I were living in Buddha. I

152

do not remember how long I remained in that state. The guide thought that I had fallen asleep, and, as it was getting late, he tried to awaken me, and so brought me back to normal consciousness.

"Later when I went to visit the temple of Viswanath [Lord Shiva] in Benares I thought to myself, 'Why have I come here? To look at a stone image?' When again the same vision! It was as if Viswanath was telling me, 'The Light is the same here as there—Truth is one.' "

Perhaps it may be of some interest to relate an experience which I myself once had during a visit to Brindavan, although it is of no great importance compared to those higher ecstatic experiences which I have just mentioned.

An American disciple, known as Sister Lalita, and I went to Brindavan by train. As we approached the station before Brindavan, the holy mantra seized my heart and lips, and in spite of myself I chanted it continuously for three days and three nights—all the time we were in Brindavan. I could not sleep a wink. And I experienced such sweetness and joy in uttering the mantra as I had never experienced before. Then, on our return journey, as we reached that station where I began to chant, the holy name left me as suddenly as it had come to me.

My master used to say, a spiritual current flows in places of pilgrimage. If an aspirant struggles a little, he can reach enlightenment easily.

There is holiness where holy people live, and where spiritual aspirants think of God and yearn to have his love and his vision. If a man thinks holy thoughts and lives a good and pure life, he not only does good to

153

himself but helps others to become good and holy. Holiness is contagious.

The deeds they perform become examples of good action.

The illumined souls are examples to be followed in every way. We should try to imitate them in all their actions. They are the guideposts to righteousness.

Some may think that, because we are not yet saints like them, we cannot follow them and imitate their actions. This is like the boy in the fable, who stood by the ocean, waiting to bathe until the waves of the ocean subsided and the ocean became calm. No. We must make an attempt to follow them, even if we only crawl. We may fall many times, but we must stand up again and again and struggle to follow in the footsteps of these great ones.

They give spiritual authority to the scriptures.

The scriptures record the experiences and teachings of the souls illumined by the knowledge of God. They are considered as authoritative only when others following in the footsteps of these illumined souls become themselves illumined.

70. *Every one of those devotees has become filled with the spirit of God.*

Their minds and wills have become identified with the mind and will of God. They are completely freed from the sense of ego that creates bondage to maya, to ignorance.

71. *When such lovers of God dwell on earth, their forefathers rejoice, the gods dance in joy, this earth becomes sanctified.*

We have seen what a great blessing these holy men are to all mankind. They sanctify the past, present, and future generations of their families; they sanctify the race and country in which they are born, and the whole world. There is a saying in the Srimad Bhagavatam, "As by watering the root of a tree, the whole tree with its branches and leaves is nourished, so by pleasing the Lord, all beings are pleased." How can one please the Lord? Love him, love him, love him.

72. *Among them there are no distinctions based on caste, learning, beauty of form, birth in a high or low family, wealth, possessions, and the like.*

73. *Because they are His own.*

Sri Ramakrishna, in this present age, emphasized the truth that there is no caste or other such distinction among the devotees of God. In fact, they belong to a caste of their own. The bodies, minds, and senses of God's devotees are equally purified. What distinction can there be among them?

When Buddha was questioned about the caste of the monks by a brahmin, he answered: "You enquire about the caste of monks, but not about their qualifications. This indeed is a delusion born of caste pride. Spiritual attainment depends only upon the mental qualifications of an aspirant, and has nothing to do with caste and so forth."

ETHICAL VIRTUES AND WORSHIP
OF GOD

74. *Arguments are to be avoided.*

75. *Because there is no end to them and they lead to*
no satisfactory result.

By arguments you get nowhere. The true spiritual
aspirants, who seek to know God, who long to love God,
do not care for vain arguments.

Arguments cannot conclusively establish the fact that
God exists. Theologians and philosophers in every
country have believed that they could prove the existence of God. But there are also many who have found
arguments to prove, to their own satisfaction, that God
does not exist.

The only proof that God is, is that one can experience
him.

Howsoever you may try to convince another person
of God's existence through arguments, he cannot be
completely satisfied.

There must arise a longing to know and experience
God, and this longing arises in the hearts of men who
have seen the vanity of earthly life.

In the Katha Upanishad it is said:

"The Self is not known through the study of the
Scriptures, nor through subtlety of the intellect, nor

through much learning. But by him who longs for him is he known. Verily unto him does the Self reveal his true being.

"By learning a man cannot know him, if he desist not from evil, if he control not his senses, if he quiet not his mind, and practice not meditation.

"Arise! Awake! Approach the feet of the Master and know That. Like the sharp edge of a razor, the sages say, is the path. Narrow it is, and difficult to tread."

In the same Upanishad the teacher tells his disciple Nachiketa:

"The awakening which thou hast known does not come through the intellect, but rather in fullest measure, from the lips of the wise. Beloved Nachiketa, blessed, blessed art thou, because thou seekest the Eternal."

If you approach a man of God with an open heart and with humility, you need no argument to convince you. As you sit before him, you do not doubt any longer that God *is*. In his presence you feel not only that God exists, but that it is possible for you to attain him.

Those of us who approached our master will testify to this truth.

76. *While you study the devotional scriptures, meditate upon their teachings and follow them so that devotion to God may be intensified in your heart.*

Study of the scriptures is necessary for beginners. Study regularly; then try to understand by meditating upon the teachings. And then live and act accordingly. Thus it is that devotion to God grows in intensity.

Once I approached Swami Turiyananda, a disciple

of Sri Ramakrishna, who was a great scholar and a knower of Brahman, and requested him to give me lessons on the Bhagavad-Gita. He agreed, and asked me to come to him the next day. He said to me, "I shall give you one lesson, the first and the last." Then he continued, "The Sanskrit of the Gita is easy to understand. Read a verse, meditate on its meaning, and then live what it teaches for a few days, before you go on to the next verse."

I have now come to understand that this is not a matter of a few days, but that if you can take one verse of the Gita and live what it teaches, you can surely become illumined in the knowledge of God.

It has been truly said by Swami Vivekananda, that if all the scriptures of the world were lost and one sentence of Christ's were left, religion would still remain alive in the world. That sentence is: "Blessed are the pure in heart, for they shall see God."

77. *It behooves a bhakta not to waste a single moment, nor to delay worshiping God until he becomes freed from pleasure and pain, from cravings and greed.*

If you wait to worship God or meditate on him until you are freed from cravings and from the pairs of opposites, such an opportunity will never arise. The waves of craving will continue to arise in your heart, but you must try to calm them and think of God and pray to him, every moment of your life.

If you give up your practice of japa or meditation merely because you do not always find peace or happiness in these practices, then you can never grow in spiritual life. Try with your whole heart to keep recollectedness of God by chanting his name and feeling his presence; your mind will gradually become calm, and you will be eventually absorbed in God and in his love.

In the Bhagavad-Gita we read: "Patiently, little by little, a man must free himself from all mental distractions, with the aid of the intelligent will. He must fix his mind upon the Atman, and never think of anything else. No matter where the restless and unquiet mind wanders, it must be drawn back and made to submit to the Atman only."

Swami Vivekananda says:

"It is very hard at first to compel the mind to think of God always, but with every new effort the power to do so grows."

In spiritual life, my master used to say, there can be no failure if we keep up the struggle.

78. *The bhakta should cultivate harmlessness, truthfulness, purity, compassion, faith, and other such virtues.*

Harmlessness. Not to hurt any creature by word, thought, or deed. This also means in a positive sense to learn to love all beings. And to love all beings becomes possible when we learn to feel the presence of God within ourselves and to feel that same presence in all.

Truthfulness. To speak without ever causing pain to another, to be truthful, to say always what is kind and beneficial.

Sri Ramakrishna used to insist on the importance of this virtue. "To be truthful is the austerity of this age," he said.

159

ETHICAL VIRTUES AND WORSHIP OF GOD

But, at the same time, we must be careful what we say, and avoid giving pain to others by uncalled for and unnecessary frankness.

Purity. External purity is cleanliness of the physical body. This is important. There is a saying, "Cleanliness is next to godliness." And it is easy to practice.

But physical purity also refers to an attitude of reverence for the teachers and seers, straightforwardness, and sexual purity.

Mental purity is even more important. The devotee must feel that when he is thinking of God and chanting his name, he is being purified by bathing in the presence of God. Regular practice is necessary in order to maintain this mental purity.

Mental purity also refers to the practice of serenity, sympathy for others, meditation upon God, and integrity of motive. Shankara declares that mental purity is freedom from attachment and aversion to the objects of the senses, while one moves among them.

Compassion. "Do unto others as you would have them do unto you."

My master taught me this truth: "Meditate, meditate, meditate. Then as you taste the bliss of God within yourself, your heart will melt in sympathy and compassion for others. You will feel how unnecessary it is for them to suffer, since there is a mine of bliss within each one of them."

Faith. Faith in the words of the scriptures and in the words of the guru. At the same time one needs faith in oneself. One must say: "Others have seen God. I also can attain him."

And other such virtues.

Sri Krishna describes these virtues in the Gita:

160

Therefore I tell you:
Be humble, be harmless,
Have no pretension,
Be upright, forbearing,
Serve your teacher
In true obedience,
Keeping the mind
And the body in cleanness,
Tranquil, steadfast,
Master of ego,
Standing apart
From the things of the senses,
Free from self;
Aware of the weakness
In mortal nature,
Its bondage to birth,
Age, suffering, dying;
To nothing be slave,
Nor desire possession
Of man-child or wife,
Of home or of household;
Calmly encounter
The painful, the pleasant;
Adore me only
With heart undistracted.
. . . .
Strive without ceasing
To know the Atman,
Seek this knowledge
And comprehend clearly
Why you should seek it:
Such, it is said,
Are the roots of true wisdom;

161

Ignorance, merely,
Is all that denies them.

79. *The blessed Lord alone is to be worshiped day and night in and through every aspect of life without any distracting thought.*

This is a state to be achieved through the practice of spiritual disciplines. In this state there is constant recollectedness of God—the current of the devotee's loving thought flows toward Him without any break or distraction. There is no longer any distinction between secular and sacred. "He who sees Brahman in every action finds Brahman." His whole life is dedicated to God, each action is prompted by his heart's devotion to God. He is free from all cares and worries.

80. *Where the Lord is worshiped thus, he soon reveals himself to the inner vision of his devotees.*

This is known as samadhi or transcendental consciousness. The spiritual eye opens, and the devotee sees the Lord within himself and within all. He lives in the bliss of God and realizes the bliss of liberation while living on earth.

81. *To love the eternal Truth—this indeed is the greatest love.*

This supreme love is also supreme wisdom.

82. *This divine love manifests itself in eleven different forms: (1) A devotee loves to chant the praises and glories of the blessed Lord. (2) He loves His enchanting beauty. (3) He loves to offer Him the*

worship of his heart. (4) He loves to meditate on His presence constantly. (5) He loves to think of himself as His servant. (6) He loves Him as his friend. (7) He loves Him as his child. (8) He loves Him as his beloved. (9) He loves to surrender himself to Him completely. (10) He loves to be completely absorbed in Him. (11) He loves to feel the pangs of separation from Him.

This last expression of love, "to feel the pangs of separation from Him," is typified in the lives of those who love God as their beloved Husband. When these pangs of separation are felt, there is also a greater bliss in union with the Beloved.

83. *These truths the teachers of bhakti unanimously declare, without being in the least afraid of public criticism. The following are known as great teachers of bhakti: Kumara, Vyasa, Suka, Shandilya, Garga, Vishnu, Kaundinya, Sesha, Uddhava, Aruni, Bali, Hanuman, Bibhisana, and many others.*

84. *Whosoever believes in this auspicious description of divine love by Narada, and has faith in these teachings, becomes a lover of God, attains the highest beatitude, and reaches the supreme goal of life.*

To have *'faith in these teachings'* implies, of course, that the teachings must be put into practice in one's own life.

I can think of no better way to conclude this commentary than to quote from a letter written by Swami

Vivekananda to two American devotees, on July 31, 1894. It is one of the most beautiful expressions I know of the spirit of bhakti yoga:

". . . catch a glimpse at least, every day, of that world of infinite beauty and peace and purity—the spiritual, and try to live in it day and night. . . . Let your souls ascend day and night like an 'unbroken string' unto the feet of the Beloved whose throne is in your own hearts and let the rest take care of themselves, that is the body and everything else. Life is evanescent, a fleeting dream; youth and beauty fade. Say day and night, 'Thou art my father, my mother, my husband, my love, my lord, my God—I want nothing but Thee, nothing but Thee. . . . Thou in me, I in Thee . . .' Wealth goes, beauty vanishes, life flies, powers fly—but the Lord abideth for ever, love abideth for ever. If here is glory in keeping the machine in good trim, it is more glorious to withhold the soul from suffering with the body—that is the only demonstration of your being 'not matter,' by letting the matter alone.

"Stick to God! Who cares what comes to the body or to anything else! Through the terrors of evil, say—my God, my love! Through the pangs of death, say—my God, my love! Through all the evils under the sun, say —my God, my love. Thou art here, I see Thee. Thou art with me, I feel Thee. I am Thine, take me. I am not of the world's but Thine, leave not then me. Do not go for glass beads leaving the mine of diamonds! This life is a great chance. What, seekest thou the pleasures of the world!—He is the fountain of all bliss. Seek for the highest, aim at that highest, and you *shall* reach the highest."

Hari Om Tat Sat.

164

GLOSSARY

acharyas. Spiritual teachers. The word is sometimes added to the name of a revered religious preceptor; *e.g.,* Shankaracharya.

Antaryamin. The Inner Ruler and Guide; an epithet of the supreme Spirit.

Atman. The Spirit or Self, the immanent aspect of the Godhead.

avatar. A divine incarnation. According to Hindu belief, God descends into the finiteness of name and form in various ages to re-establish the forgotten truths of religion and to show mankind by his living example how to ascend to himself.

avidya. Ignorance. Philosophically speaking, avidya is individual ignorance, and *maya* is universal ignorance.

Bhagavad-Gita or *Gita.* Lit., "Song of God," it is the gospel of Hinduism. Dated between the fifth and second centuries B.C., the Gita, which comprises eighteen chapters, is a part of the *Mahabharata.* In the form of a dialogue between Sri Krishna, the divine incarnation, and his friend and disciple, Arjuna, it teaches how to achieve union with the supreme Reality through the paths of knowledge, devotion, selfless work, and meditation.

bhakta. A devotee of God.

bhakti. Devotion to God.

bhakti yoga. The path of devotion; one of the four main yogas, or paths to union with God. After cultivating love for one of the many aspects of God as a personal being—often as a divine incarnation—the worshiper ultimately merges his own ego in his *Chosen Ideal.*

bhava. Matured *bhakti.*

brahmachari. 1. A spiritual aspirant who has taken the first monastic vows. 2. An individual devoted to continence and other religious practices in observance of the first of the four stages of life according to Vedic teachings.

Brahman. The impersonal absolute Existence or Godhead, the all-pervading transcendental Reality of *Vedanta* philosophy. See also *maya.*

165

Brahmananda, Swami. Rakhal Chandra Ghosh, 1863-1922, a monastic disciple of Sri *Ramakrishna* whom the latter regarded as his spiritual son. He was for many years head of the Ramakrishna Order. A great saint and spiritual teacher, he transformed the life and character of many.

brahmin. Referring to the brahmin caste. As described in the *Gita*, the idea of caste refers to a natural order—determined by a man's *karma* and predominating *guna*. The brahmin caste includes priests, pandits, philosophers, and religious leaders.

Chaitanya. One of the great religious figures of Hinduism, born in Bengal in 1485. According to Bengal Vaishnavas, Sri Chaitanya was a divine incarnation of Krishna. His ecstatic love of God embraced sinners and saints, regardless of caste and creed. Sri Chaitanya stressed *bhakti yoga* as a way to God-realization with special emphasis on *japa* as a spiritual practice.

Chandi. A sacred text in praise of the Divine Mother.

Chosen Ideal (*Ishta*, in Sanskrit). The aspect of the Godhead selected by a spiritual aspirant, or by his *guru* for him. Through meditation on his Chosen Ideal, the aspirant gradually attains concentration of mind, love of God, and ultimately illumination. See also *mantra*.

cycle (*yuga*, in Sanskrit). One of the four ages into which the duration of the world is divided according to Hindu mythology. In the first period, righteousness is predominant, but with each succeeding age virtue diminishes and evil increases. At the end of the fourth age (through which the world is said to be passing at present), the whole cycle begins again with the first age.

darshan. Lit., "seeing, experiencing"; paying respects to a holy place or person by a ceremonial visit; also the blessing or purification felt in the presence of holiness.

dasya. The devotee's attitude toward God of servant to Master or of child to Parent.

diksha. Initiation of an aspirant into spiritual life by a *guru*.

gauni bhakti. Preparatory devotion, which leads ultimately to the supreme love of God. See *para bhakti*.

Gayatri. 1. The sacred Vedic *mantra*: "May we meditate on the effulgent Light of him who is worshipful, and who has given birth to all worlds. May we direct the rays of our intelligence toward the path of good." 2. The presiding deity of the Gayatri mantra.

Gita. See *Bhagavad-Gita.*

gopi. A milkmaid of Brindavan. The gopis were companions and devotees of Sri Krishna. Examples of the most intense divine love, they were considered by Sri Ramakrishna to have been saints or seers (rishis) in an earlier incarnation.

guna. Any one of three types of energies: *sattva, rajas,* and *tamas.* The three gunas make up the universe of mind and matter. When the gunas are in perfect balance, there is no creation, expression, or manifestation. When the balance is disturbed, creation occurs.

guru. A spiritual teacher. A qualified guru is, ideally, an illumined soul, or well advanced on the religious path. Swami *Vivekananda* said that a guru must know the spirit of the scriptures; he must be sinless; and he must teach selflessly, without desire for name, fame, or wealth. A competent guru assumes responsibility for the spiritual life of his disciple and leads him to salvation.

Hari Om Tat Sat. Lit., "That is Being"; sacred syllables used to invoke the presence of God.

homa. A ceremony dating from Vedic times, in which oblations are offered into a fire built according to scriptural injunctions. The fire is considered to be the visible manifestation of the deity worshiped. The homa is a ritual of inner purification, at the end of which the devotee makes a mental offering to the deity of all his thoughts, words, actions and their fruits.

initiation. The ceremony (*diksha,* in Sanskrit) which symbolizes the beginning of spiritual life. During initiation the *guru* gives his disciple specific instructions in spiritual practices—more particularly a *mantra.* The usual form of diksha is by mantra. Two other forms of diksha, given only by *avatars* or *Ishvarakotis,* are effected by the mere wish, look, or touch of the guru. Initiation may also refer to ceremonies of acceptance into monastic life—either *brahmacharya* or *sannyas.*

Ishta. See *Chosen Ideal.*

Ishvarakoti. One belonging to a class of eternally free and perfect souls, born on earth for the good of mankind. According to Sri *Ramakrishna*, an Ishvarakoti has several of the characteristics of an *avatar*.

japa, also japam. The practice of repeating one of God's names—usually one's own *mantra.* A rosary may be used to facilitate counting a required amount.

jivanmukta. One who has attained liberation from *karma* and reincarnation through union with God while living in the physical body.

jnana. 1. Knowledge. 2. Knowledge of the ultimate Reality; the transcendental realization that *Atman* and *Brahman* are one.

jnana yoga. See *yoga.*

jnani. 1. One who follows the path of knowledge and discrimination to reach the impersonal Reality; a nondualist. 2. A knower of *Brahman.*

Kali. A name of the Divine Mother. Kali is usually pictured as dancing on the chest of the inert *Shiva,* her husband, who symbolizes the transcendent aspect of Spirit whereas she symbolizes the dynamic aspect, the Primal Energy. Wearing a girdle of severed arms and a necklace of skulls, Kali holds the bleeding head of a demon in her lower left hand, a sword in the upper left. She makes the sign of fearlessness with the upper right hand and offers boons with the lower right—destroying ignorance, preserving world order, and blessing and liberating those who yearn for God-realization. Kali is the deity of the famous temple at Dakshineswar, and was worshiped there for many years by Sri *Ramakrishna.*

kanta. Lit., "husband"; the attitude of the devotee toward God as of wife or lover toward Husband or Beloved.

karma. A mental or physical act; the consequences of an individual's actions in this and previous lives; the chain of cause and effect operating in the moral world.

karma yoga. See *yoga.*

liberation. See *moksha.*

lila. The divine play, in which the same actor—God—enacts all roles, so to speak. The whole universe is said to be created by him as sport, for his pleasure. A special manifestation of lila is the *avatar*. Lila, moreover, means relativity (which consists of time, space, and causation).

loka. Sphere or plane of existence.

Madhava. Lit., "the Sweet One," a name of God.

madhura. The attitude toward God of wife or lover to Husband or Beloved.

Mahabharata. Perhaps the world's longest epic poem, consisting of some 100,000 couplets—including the *Bhagavad-Gita*. Its earliest composition has been estimated at no later than the fifth century B.C. Expanding upon and illustrating the truths of the *Vedas*, the Mahabharata tells the story of King Bharata's descendants—the Pandavas and Kauravas. According to Vyasa, the reputed author of the epic, the purpose of the Mahabharata is to sing the glory of God, the dynastic war between the Pandavas and Kauravas merely providing the occasion.

mahabhava. The highest manifestation of divine love.

mantra, also mantram. 1. The particular name of God, corresponding to the *Chosen Ideal* of the disciple, with which the latter is initiated into spiritual life by his *guru*. The mantra, regarded as one with God, represents the essence of the guru's instructions to his disciple, who is enjoined to keep it sacred and secret, and to meditate for the rest of his life on the aspect of God which it symbolizes. Repetition of the mantra (*japa*), performed regularly and reverently, results in purification of the mind and ultimately in God-realization. 2. Sacred word, verse, or Vedic hymn.

maya. A universal principle of *Vedanta* philosophy; the basis of mind and matter. Maya is *Brahman's* power; in this sense maya is inseparable from Brahman, as heat is inseparable from fire. United, Brahman and maya constitute the Personal God, who creates, preserves, and dissolves the universe. In another sense, as Ignorance, or Cosmic Illusion, maya is a superimposition upon Brahman. Maya veils man's vision of Brahman, as a result of which man perceives the manifold universe instead of the one Reality. Maya has two aspects: *avidya* (ignorance) and *vidya* (knowledge). Avidya-maya leads man into greater worldliness and bondage and is expressed in passions and cravings. Vidya-maya leads man toward the realization of Brahman

169

and expresses itself in spiritual virtues. Both vidya and avidya are within relativity (time, space, and causation); man transcends vidya and avidya when he realizes Brahman, the Absolute.

moha. Delusion.

moksha. Final liberation from *karma* and reincarnation—*i.e.*, from all worldly bondage—through union with God or knowledge of the ultimate Reality.

Naren. See *Vivekananda.*

nativadi. Lit., "one who does not talk too much." In the *Upanishads*, nativadi refers to a characteristic of the illumined soul. Shankara explains the word as meaning "one who is humble and does not assert himself."

nirvana. The state of spiritual enlightenment or transcendental consciousness, characterized by extinction or absorption of the individual and ephemeral ego in *Brahman.*

nirvikalpa samadhi. A term of *Vedanta* philosophy referring to the transcendental state of consciousness, in which the spiritual aspirant becomes completely absorbed in *Brahman* so that all sense of duality is obliterated.

Om, sometimes spelled Aum. The sacred syllable represents the impersonal Absolute as well as the personal aspect of God; the Logos. Om is the undifferentiated Word which has produced all manifestation. Repetition of Om with meditation on its meaning is prescribed as an effective spiritual practice.

para bhakti. Supreme love of God.

prakriti. One of two ultimate realities postulated by Sankhya philosophy. Prakriti denotes primordial nature; it is composed of three *gunas* and constitutes the material of the universe. By its proximity to *Purusha,* prakriti evolves as the world of mind and matter.

prarabdha karma. The portion of stored-up *karma* from past lives which has begun to bear fruit in the present life, in which it must be exhausted.

prasad. Food or any other gift which has been ceremonially offered to God or to a saintly person.

prema. Ecstatic love of God.

170

GLOSSARY

Purana. Lit., "ancient"; any one of eighteen sacred books of Hinduism, attributed to Vyasa, which elaborate and popularize the spiritual truths of the *Vedas* by means of illustrations from the lives of divine incarnations, saints, kings, and devotees, whether historical or mythological.

Purusha. One of the two ultimate realities postulated by Sankhya philosophy. Purusha denotes the Self, the Absolute, Spirit, pure Consciousness. It is the witness of the changes of *prakriti.*

raja yoga. See *yoga.*

rajas. Activity, restlessness. See *guna.*

Rama. One of the most popular divine incarnations of Hinduism, king of Ayodhya, and hero of the Ramayana (one of India's most famous epics).

Ramakrishna. 1836-1886, a God-man of unique spiritual capacity. Sri Ramakrishna spent most of his adult life near Calcutta, living in the grounds of a temple on the bank of the Ganges. After realizing his union with God through various paths within Hinduism, as well as through Christianity and Islam, Sri Ramakrishna proclaimed that the ultimate Reality can be known by a follower of any religion if his devotion is equal to the task. Already during his lifetime, Sri Ramakrishna was accorded divine worship. Since his passing away he has received widespread recognition as an incarnation of God. A monastic order was founded in Sri Ramakrishna's name, devoted to God-realization as well as to service of God in man.

sadhana. The practice of spiritual disciplines.

sakhya. The devotee's attitude toward God of friend to Friend.

samadhi. 1. The superconscious state in which man experiences his identity with the ultimate Reality. 2. Absorption, the eighth limb of *raja yoga,* in which the mind takes on the form of the object of meditation. It is defined by Patanjali as a state in which "the true nature of the object shines forth, not distorted by the mind of the perceiver."

samskara. An impression, tendency, or potentiality, created in the mind of an individual as a result of an action or thought. The sum total of a man's samskaras represents his character. See also *karma.*

171

NARADA'S WAY OF DIVINE LOVE

sandhya. Worship and meditation performed at dawn, noon, and sunset, by orthodox Hindus.

sannyas. 1. The monastic life, dedicated to the practice of complete renunciation of self and to the attainment of knowledge of the supreme Reality. 2. Initiation during which the monastic aspirant takes the final vows of renunciation; also the status of one who has taken such vows.

Sarada Devi. Saradamani Mukhopadhyaya, also known as the Holy Mother, 1853-1920, wife of Sri *Ramakrishna.* Their married life was characterized by unbroken continence, showing the highest ideals of the householder and of the monastic ways of life. Although the Holy Mother tried to hide her extraordinary spiritual gifts under the guise of a simple country woman, she is accorded worship—and was, even during her lifetime—as an incarnation of the Divine Mother.

Sat-chit-ananda. Absolute Existence, absolute Consciousness, absolute Bliss—an epithet of *Brahman.*

sattva. The quality of purity and harmony. See *guna.*

savikalpa samadhi. The first stage of transcendental consciousness, in which the distinction between subject and object persists. In this state the spiritual aspirant may have a mystic vision of the Personal God, with or without form.

Self. 1. The *Atman.* 2. (lower case) the ego.

Shakti. God as Mother of the Universe; personification of the Primal Energy or power of *Brahman.* She is the dynamic aspect of the Godhead, that which creates, preserves, and dissolves the universe; in relation to which *Shiva* represents Brahman (the transcendental Absolute, or father aspect of the Godhead).

Shankara, also Shankaracharya. One of the greatest philosopher-saints of India, chief exponent of nondualistic *Vedanta.* The dates assigned to him vary from the sixth to the eighth century, A.D. During his brief life of thirty-two years, Shankara organized a system of monastic denominations which is still in existence today. His enormous literary output includes commentaries on the Vedanta Sutras, the principal *Upanishads,* and the *Gita;* two major philosophical works, the Upadeshasahasri

172

and the Vivekachudamani, and many poems, hymns, prayers, and minor works on Vedanta.

shanta. The attitude of peace and serenity, in which God is felt near but no definite relationship has been established between him and the worshiper.

Shiva. God in his aspect of Dissolver, one of the Hindu Trinity. When worshiped as the *Chosen Ideal*, Shiva is regarded as the total Godhead, the supreme Reality. In relation to his power—the dynamic creative mother aspect of God *(Shakti)*, Shiva is the transcendent Absolute, or father aspect. Shiva is also worshiped as the *guru* of all gurus—destroyer of worldliness, giver of wisdom, and embodiment of renunciation and compassion.

shraddha. Faith in the words of the guru and the scriptures.

siddha. 1. A perfected soul. 2. One who has occult powers. 3. A semi-divine spirit.

Sri. 1. Meaning "revered" or "holy"; used as a prefix to honor a deity, or a holy personality, or a sacred book. 2. The Hindu equivalent of the English "Mr." 3. A name of Lakshmi, the Divine Mother.

Srimad Bhagavatam. One of the great religious classics of the world, in which legends about Sri Krishna and the early sages popularize truths from the *Vedas.*

Sutasamhita. A collection of Vedic *mantras* or hymns.

tamas. Lit., "darkness"; see *guna.*

triputi bheda. The untying of the three knots of knowledge, which consist of the subject, the object, and the process of knowledge. When the three knots are untied, the spiritual aspirant attains unitary consciousness.

Turiya. The superconscious; lit., "the Fourth," in relation to the three ordinary states of consciousness—waking, dreaming, and dreamless sleep which it transcends.

Upanishads. The sacred scriptures which constitute the philosophical portion of the *Vedas.* The Upanishads teach the knowledge of God and record the spiritual experiences of the sages of ancient India. Since the Upanishads brought to a close each of the four Vedas, they became known as *Vedanta—anta* or "end" of the Vedas.

vairagya. Dispassion, renunciation.

vatsalya. The devotee's attitude toward God of parent toward Child.

Vedanta. Lit., "end of the Veda." A religious philosophy which has evolved from the teachings of the latter or knowledge portion of the *Vedas* (the *Upanishads*). In this sense, it is the common basis of all religious sects of India. Through all its various shades—dualistic, qualified nondualistic, pluralistic, realistic, and nondualistic, Vedanta teaches that the purpose of man's life is to realize the ultimate Reality, or Godhead, here and now, through spiritual practice. Vedanta accepts all the great spiritual teachers and personal or impersonal aspects of the Godhead worshiped by different religions, considering them as manifestations of the one Reality. By demonstrating the essential unity at the source of all religions, Vedanta serves as a framework within which all spiritual truth may be expressed. Vedanta is often, but less correctly, called Hinduism, a word first used by the Persians for the inhabitants of India, because they lived on the far side of the river Sindhu, or Indus.

Vedas. The most ancient scriptures of the Hindus, regarded by the orthodox as direct divine revelation and supreme authority in all religious matters. There are four Vedas—the Rik, the Sama, the Yajus, and the Atharva—each consisting of a ritual or "work" portion and a philosophical or "knowledge" portion. Each knowledge portion comprises *Upanishads.*

vidya. Knowledge. See *maya.*

vina. A large plucked stringed instrument of India, with a bowl-shaped body carved from a single piece of wood, and a long neck curved downward at the end with a gourd attached to the underside.

Vishnu. Lit., "the all-pervading"; God as the Preserver, one of the Hindu Trinity. Among the many forms of Vishnu, a familiar one is his four-armed aspect, in which he is seen holding a discus, a mace, a conchshell, and a lotus. According to the doctrine of *avatar,* Vishnu appears on earth when needed for the good of the world.

Vivekananda, Swami. Narendranath Datta, 1863-1902, monastic disciple and chief apostle of Sri *Ramakrishna.* He was known as Naren or Narendra, and later as Swamiji. In 1893 he rep-

GLOSSARY

resented Hinduism at the World's Parliament of Religions in Chicago and in 1899 he made a second trip to the West, lecturing and establishing *Vedanta* centers. He was a leader of the monastic brotherhood (the Ramakrishna Math) and founded the Ramakrishna Mission. Vivekananda is considered to have been the interpreter of Vedanta in this modern age. But more than that, he was a saint of the highest order, dedicated to the worship of God in every being.

yoga. The act of yoking or joining. 1. Union of the individual soul with the Godhead. 2. The method by which such union is achieved. The several methods include *bhakti yoga,* the path of devotion; *jnana yoga,* the path of discrimination between the eternal and the noneternal; *karma yoga,* the path of selfless action, and *raja yoga,* the path of meditation (a means of attaining the highest consciousness and final release from worldly bondages by control of the mind).

BOOKS CONSULTED

Aphorisms on the Gospel of Divine Love or Narada Bhakti Sutras.
Translated with commentary by Swami Tyagishananda.
Madras: Ramakrishna Math, 1955.

Bhaktiprasanga (in Bengali), by Swami Vedantananda.
Calcutta: Model Publishing House.

The Holy Bible.

The Gospel of Sri Ramakrishna, by M. Translated by Swami
Nikhilananda. New York: Ramakrishna-Vivekananda Center,
1942.

Gospel of Ramakrishna. Revised by Swami Abhedananda from
M's original English text. New York: Vedanta Society, 1947.

Inspired Talks, by Swami Vivekananda. Mayavati: Advaita Ash-
rama.

Bhagavad-Gita: Song of God. Translated by Swami Prabhavananda and Christopher Isherwood. Hollywood: Vedanta Press,
1951; New York: New American Library, 1954.

The Upanishads. Translated by Swami Prabhavananda and
Frederick Manchester. Hollywood: Vedanta Press, 1947; New
York: New American Library, 1957.

Ramakrishna and His Disciples, by Christopher Isherwood. New
York: Simon and Schuster, 1965.

Vivekachudamani—Shankara's Crest-Jewel of Discrimination.
Translated by Swami Prabhavananda and Christopher Isher-
wood. Hollywood: Vedanta Press, 1947; New York: New
American Library, 1970.

Srimad Bhagavatam: The Wisdom of God. Translated by Swami
Prabhavananda. New York: G. Putnam and Co., 1943.

The Way of a Pilgrim and the Pilgrim Continues His Way.
Translated by R. M. French. London: Society for Promoting
Christian Knowledge, 1965.

How to Know God, the Yoga Aphorisms of Patanjali. Translated
with a new commentary by Swami Prabhavananda and Christopher Isherwood. Hollywood: Vedanta Press, 1953; New York:
New American Library, 1969.